Think
like a
PHILOSOPHER

Think like a PHILOSOPHER

Get to grips with reasoning
and ethics

Anne Rooney

This edition published in 2019 by Arcturus Publishing Limited
26/27 Bickels Yard, 151–153 Bermondsey Street,
London SE1 3HA

AD006841UK

Printed in the UK

CONTENTS

What is philosophy for?

Some people think of philosophy as an ivory-tower occupation with no application to the real world. They couldn't be more wrong. Philosophy lies behind every important decision we make and affects all aspects of our lives.

Philosophical thought has created our laws and our interpretations of religious texts. The way we treat criminals, how we structure our schools, the placing of CCTV cameras, the presence of GM ingredients in our foodstuffs, how much tax we pay, the availability of porn online, and whether we can have an organ transplant are all philosophical issues.

Thinking about ethical, political and metaphysical questions is enjoyable and empowering. It is essential if you want to develop informed views on the critical questions of modern life.

Philosophy will help you to work out what you think and why, and enable you to become the type of person you believe you should be. This doesn't mean fulfilling an ambition to become a film star or astronaut – it means knowing what is important to you and living your life by your own set of standards and priorities. There can be no more important or satisfying aim, no better work than person-building, and no better place to start than with yourself and your own brain.

Lots of questions – are there any answers?

If we want to know which of two mountains is taller, we can measure them both and compare the results. If we measure accurately, we will have a definitive answer.

Philosophy is not like that. If you say there is a God and I say there is not a God, we can both present our reasons for thinking as we do but there is no way an objective observer can be certain who is right.

We have no way of finding a universally 'true' answer to questions such as the morality of abortion, or whether democracy is the fairest form of government.

Philosophers traditionally drink too much alcohol and coffee, smoke too much and stress over the meaning of life.

'What I really lack is to be clear in my mind what I am to do ... the thing is to find a truth which is true for me, to find the idea for which I can live and die.'

Søren Kierkegaard, 1835

With no equivalent of the tape-measure-for-measuring-mountains, how can we test our ideas? We can work out through reasoned discussion which of two or more conflicting ideas is preferable. To gain anything, you must come to philosophy with an open mind and a desire to learn, to change or deepen your views. You may, in the end, find you still hold the same views but they will have a stronger foundation as they will be rooted in reason and supported by evidence.

Opinion vs truth

Because there are no definitive, external proofs, some people are inclined to think that philosophical questions are just a matter of opinion. But the lack of 'right' answers doesn't make a question a matter of opinion. Instead, philosophy consists of setting forth propositions and exploring or defending them through logic and reasoned argument, refuting counter-arguments, and trying to edge towards the best possible answers.

These answers might well be overthrown by another argument – just as a theory in physics might later be replaced by a better theory. In physics, a preferred theory is one that better fits the observed phenomena and enables us to make predictions which turn out to be accurate. For an idea to be sound in philosophy, it must be consistent, without internal contradiction, inclusive, and, in many cases, universally applicable.

Is it ever true?
If we can't conclusively demonstrate the truth of a philosophical statement, does that mean we can't say there are philosophical truths? This is a question philosophers have asked, and – as you might expect – they have come up with different answers.

Few philosophers would argue that the murder of innocent civilians in times of war can ever be justified. Viewed from a modern perspective, the Austro-Hungarian army's summary execution of Serbs during World War I was clearly a war crime.

The question is not limited to philosophy: it is also asked of other disciplines, including physics. Are our discoveries in physics really discoveries of an objective truth, or are they just a convenient way of representing our observations of the world? It is possible that the truth is 'out there', but we can't be sure.

'Killing people is wrong'

Like science, philosophy tries to approach the truth. If we take the statement 'killing people is wrong', we can quickly come up with cases in which some people might not think it wrong – when a terminally ill person in pain asks for release, for example. This makes the proposition not universally applicable,

DANGER – PHILOSOPHERS AT WORK

The Ancient Greek philosopher Socrates wandered around Athens, teaching philosophy. His frequent debates with the aristocratic youth annoyed the city elders, who saw him making young people more troublesome and argumentative than they needed to be. He was eventually put on trial for corrupting the young and offending the gods. Offered the chance of a reprieve if he would give up philosophy, Socrates refused, further antagonizing the court. He was sentenced to death and took his own life under duress in 399BC by drinking hemlock, surrounded by his friends. He is considered the originator of Western philosophy.

Persecution is a perennial danger for philosophers. Totalitarian regimes often turn against the intellectuals in their midst. Mao's China, Pol Pot's Cambodia and Stalin's USSR all imprisoned and abused intellectuals because of their dangerous potential to encourage the populace to challenge the authorities. The same accusation had been levelled at Socrates 2,500 years previously. People who don't think are easy to govern and easy to oppress. Philosophers are the intellectual equivalent of arms dealers in the eyes of an unenlightened state.

so it needs to be adjusted. We could refine it to 'killing people against their wishes is wrong'. Again, we might come up with objections. What about war? What about judicial execution? Some people will still hold that the very first statement is true, and could provide arguments to support their view, but others might amend the statement again, perhaps to 'killing innocent people against their wishes in peacetime is wrong'.

Through this process of scrutiny and iteration, philosophy tries to come up with rules and beliefs by which we can live, build societies and relate honestly to the natural world. Perhaps, along the way, it might also discover some truths.

CHAPTER 1

How do you know how to think?

What is the best way to proceed with philosophical thought?

Question everything

Disciplined thinking takes nothing for granted. In the last chapter, we saw that the apparently simple question – which of two mountains is taller? – needs to be more clearly defined before it can be answered. In philosophy, all questions and all terms must be examined and defined before we can feel secure in proposing answers.

> '*Philosophy is a discipline. You've got to discipline your thought. It's not just making stuff up. And disciplining your thought is very hard to achieve.*'
>
> Tim Crane, Knightbridge Professor of Philosophy, University of Cambridge

The tools we use for philosophy are logic and reason; the arguments they produce can only be presented in language. This means that language itself falls under scrutiny. A good part of the philosophical work of the 20th century went into examining the foundations and reliability of language.

When you begin to look at philosophy, it can feel as if everything is constantly shifting, and questions multiply in front of you. It can be invigorating, or terrifying, or both. If you like certainty, philosophy might not be for you. But if you enjoy mental gymnastics and don't mind the ground you have built your life on being wrenched from beneath your feet, it might be just what you're looking for.

Dismantling certainty

Socrates said the only thing he was sure about was his own ignorance, and if he was wiser than other men it was because he recognized his ignorance. Socrates challenged people who thought themselves knowledgeable by asking them to define common concepts such as 'courage' or 'justice'. He would then present counter-arguments, revealing inconsistencies or contradictions in whatever they said – it didn't matter how they answered, he could always pick holes in their argument. Socrates intended to show that everything is more complicated than we are inclined to think, and accepting commonly-held beliefs without scrutiny is unwise. That was how he fell out of favour with the authorities in Athens. His way of teaching, known as the Socratic method, is still used. It is a dialectic method – a dialogue framed as a reasoned argument in which logical responses should lead the participants to the 'truth'.

A fractal is a pattern that becomes ever more complex. The pattern replicates as it fragments, so you can see smaller and smaller details the closer you look at it. In mathematics, the area enclosed by a fractal is finite but has a boundary of infinite length. You can think of philosophy as fractal – every question leads on to further questions.

Thesis-building

Although Socrates used dialectic principally to unpick established beliefs, it has been used since his day to build knowledge. Again it works through a process of questions and answers, the answers prompting new questions that probe further and allow the participants to edge towards a deeper understanding.

Dialectic is often associated with the 18th-century German philosopher Georg Hegel (pictured above), who presented it in a threefold manner:

- **thesis:** the idea or statement being proposed as true, such as 'lying is wrong'
- **antithesis:** a reasoned answer to the thesis, contradicting it, such as 'lying sometimes protects people from harm; therefore it can be good'
- **synthesis:** a new statement of the idea, revised in the light of the objections raised by the antithesis. In our example, it might be 'lying when it is not intended to protect the person being lied to is wrong'.

The process can be repeated. The synthesis becomes the new thesis, and is examined and readjusted. By going through these steps, either in dialogue with someone else or by thinking the argument through yourself, you can scrutinize your ideas and make them more robust.

Court cases are tried by debate, with one side arguing in favour of the defendant and the other arguing the case for the prosecution. Skills and methods of philosophical debate are used to determine whether or not someone is guilty of the crime.

Start from scratch

In general, philosophers start with the work of earlier philosophers and use logic and argument to move the debate forwards. But this is not always the case. Philosophy is one of a few disciplines in which it's possible to throw out baby and bathwater and run a new bath, starting from first principles. As long as the new model is logical and internally consistent, it stands a fighting chance of being taken seriously.

Martin Heidegger (1889–1976) and Ludwig Wittgenstein (1889–1951) both decided that for two thousand years, philosophers had got it all wrong and it was time to start again. Wittgenstein even stated: 'It is a matter of indifference to me whether the thoughts that I have had have been anticipated by someone else.' It certainly saves a lot of time that would otherwise be spent reading up on previous ideas, and can bring a freshness that allows completely new angles to emerge.

The role of logic

Logic is a highly formalized way of thinking and reasoning that involves using language as a precision tool. The first philosopher to set out the methods of logic was Aristotle, who lived in Athens in 384–322BC. He showed how we can start with two true statements that share one 'term', and draw another true statement from them using the terms they don't share. The most famous example of this method – called logical syllogism – is:

All men are mortal. Socrates is a man. *Therefore* Socrates is mortal.

Here, the shared term is 'men/man' – it's in the first two statements. Let's reduce it to something more formulaic:

All As are B. C is an A. *Therefore* C is B.

The third statement remains true even when we remove the content (the details of men and mortality). This shows that the

logic is valid: it is a formal relationship between statements. As long as the first two statements are true, the sequence will always work. Logic of this kind cannot be refuted – the difficulty for philosophy is filling in the terms (finding the statements) – that lead to useful and meaningful conclusions. This is where we need to be very precise and careful.

Suppose we were to say:

Killing people is wrong. Abortion involves killing people. *Therefore* abortion is wrong.

This is open to several challenges. The first is whether 'killing people is wrong' is a true statement – there might be circumstances in which killing people is not wrong. The second is whether abortion involves killing people: we have to ask when or whether a foetus counts as a person, and whether we can 'kill' something that is not independently alive. Although the logic is sound, the content is not. To practise philosophy, you need to keep a tight rein on both logic and content – to 'discipline your thought'.

Where to start?

The French philosopher René Descartes (who, incidentally, also invented the Cartesian coordinate system used to draw graphs) famously said: 'I think, therefore I am.' It was his starting point for philosophy. He realized that he needed to start from something he could feel sure of, a secure proposition.

The position of certainty he came up with was his own existence, proved by his being able to think. Using Aristotle's system of syllogisms, he could say:

Only things that exist can think. I can think.
Therefore **I exist.**

We now know that the first statement is a moot point – do all microorganisms think, for example? – so Descartes was possibly basing his supposition on flawed logic.

For most people, the more important and pressing questions in philosophy are ethical – these are concerned with what is morally right and wrong. This is the area where we are most likely to encounter philosophical quandaries in our daily lives, and where they will impact on actions. Questions such as whether we should move an elderly relative into residential care against her wishes, or how we should treat animals, probably seem more relevant than if/why anything exists.

Often this is where you will start – asking what you should do, or trying to decide your opinion on a topical issue. But philosophical questions are especially prone to mission creep. Something that starts off as a seemingly straightforward and specific question often has roots that go far deeper – which is why Descartes had to start by establishing that he existed. It is precisely this aspect that makes philosophy so fascinating and rewarding.

CHAPTER 2

What do we mean by 'reality'?

If a tree falls in the forest and there is no one to hear it, does it make a sound?

What do we mean by reality? Does anything exist? Can we be sure? And is existing the same as being real?

What is out there?

For a philosopher, nothing is given – we have to prove things, and that includes proving existence. Descartes came up with his

> 'What is comprehended by you or I may not be [comprehended] by a cat, for example. If a tree falls in a park and there is no one to hand, it is silent and invisible and nameless. And if we were to vanish, there would be no tree at all; any meaning would vanish along with us. Other than what the cats make of it all, of course.'
>
> William Fossett,
> *Natural States*, 1754

THE TREE QUESTION

If a tree falls over in a forest and there is no one around, does it make a sound? It's a commonly cited philosophical question. The 17th-century philosopher John Locke would have said the answer is no. Most scientists would agree: 'sound' is defined by being heard. As the tree falls it creates vibrations in the air which are experienced as sound if a hearing observer is present. If you wave your hand in the air it makes vibrations of the same type as the falling tree or a ringing bell. But the air is moving so slowly that we can't hear the hand waving, hence the silence. It's possible that some other creature might be able to hear the sound of a waving hand. For them, the world would be a very noisy place.

famous saying, 'I think therefore I am', during his attempt to establish what he could be sure of. He felt secure in his own existence because he believed he couldn't be thinking unless he existed. But his assumption is not secure. Later philosophers pointed out that all thinking proved was that thinking was occurring – not that Descartes existed to do it.

Even if you feel secure in your existence, can you be sure that anyone else exists? Perhaps you have created the

entire external world with
all its people and your past
experiences (and this book, to
prompt you to think about it).
Perhaps nothing else is real.

Real or idea?

Philosophers who believe reality exists independently of any observers are called realists. Those who think reality is an idea constructed in the human mind are idealists. There are plenty of shades of realism and idealism.

The most fundamental realism holds that everything exists and is just as it appears to us. This is the default position for most people – we live our daily lives with the assumption that reality is 'out there' and is how we think it is. Philosophers call this 'naïve realism'. Aristotle was an arch-realist – he felt secure that the world 'out there' existed and was real. He also believed that our senses give us a reliable experience of the world. Plato, Aristotle's tutor, had a more complicated view. He believed that there were two tiers of 'reality'. One, the superior tier, was the realm of ideal 'forms'. The form is the essence or ideal of something – the perfect horse, the most complete conception of justice, even the best haircut all exist as 'forms'.

Unfortunately, the realm of forms is not accessible to us in our imperfect bodies. Instead we dwell in the second tier of reality, the rather shoddy material world. Here there are lots of instances (or instantiations) of the forms, but none is very good. The horses aren't super-sleek and super-fast, the justice systems are a bit corrupt, and there are a lot of bad hairstyles. But it's the only reality accessible to us, so we'll have to make do with it. Plato used the allegory of the cave (see page 24) to try to explain the disparity between what we perceive as reality (the material world) and the purer, high-grade realm of forms.

THE ALLEGORY OF THE CAVE

Imagine a group of people held prisoner in a cave. On the wall, they can see shadows cast by creatures outside the cave. As far as the people inside the cave are concerned, these shadows are real. They come up with theories to explain how reality works and why things are as they are (= appear to be). If one person were to escape from the cave and see real reality, they would struggle with it at first. On their return to the cave they would have great difficulty explaining to the other cave-dwellers that what they could see on the wall was not reality at all. Plato adopts the role of the returned fugitive trying to explain this philosophical idea to humanity: that what we see is not top-notch reality, even though it is all we can experience.

The German philosopher Immanuel Kant (1724–1804) took a similar approach, distinguishing between objects we experience as *phenomena* – visible, graspable, smellable, apprehendible reality – and objects 'things in themselves', which he called *noumena*. These *noumena* don't appear in space and time and we cannot apprehend them because they exist independently of human sense/perception.

> '*The reality of external objects does not admit of strict proof.*'
>
> Immanuel Kant, 1781

Alternative (non)-realities

If you're not convinced that reality exists, there are other options to choose from, including:

- **'Brain in a vat'** – you are not really a brain in a body that is walking around. You are a brain which is kept somewhere in a vat of sustaining fluid. Your brain is fed images and sensations by a computer that has created a virtual reality which you now believe is real.

- **'The evil demon'** – an evil demon has you in his control and is persuading you that 'reality' is real.
- **'It's all a dream'** – dreams seem real when we experience them, so how do we know that all our life is not a dream? In the 4th century BC, Chinese philosopher Zhuangzi reported dreaming that he was a butterfly. On waking, he asked how he could know which identity was real: was he Zhuangzi dreaming he was a butterfly, or a butterfly dreaming he was Zhuangzi?
- ***The Matrix* is true** – we are inhabiting a computer simulation created by some other beings.
- **'It just happened'** – the world was created very recently, perhaps last Thursday. (The theory is sometimes called Last Thursdayism.) Everything in it, including your memories, has been created to give the impression that it is much older. This is a slightly shorter-term version of Creationism, which maintains that the world was created, with its apparent geological history, only a few thousand years ago.

There is no way of proving that things which seem to be very old were not created recently, and endowed with compelling evidence of their antiquity in order to deceive us.

Putting God in the frame

The Anglo-Irish bishop George Berkeley (1685–1753), who is often falsely credited with asking the tree question (see page 22), would have said that not only is there no sound, there is also no tree. But there is no tree in rather a special sense.

For Berkeley, as later for William Fossett, all experience is perceived through our senses. Everything that exists is simply our perception of things and states, internal and external. If we don't perceive it, it doesn't exist; or 'Esse is percipi' – to be is to be perceived. But Berkeley didn't believe we constructed all these sense perceptions from nothing. As he said, when we open our eyes, we don't choose what to see. The variety of perceptions comes from God. And as God continues to see a tree even when no one else is looking, the tree continues in the same place for the next person who comes along. It's a clever theory, but it demands a lot of God – not least of all, his existence.

What are things like?

What we can know of things that exist is always mediated through our bodies – either our senses or our minds (see

Chapter 3). Again, we are thrown back on perceptions. We describe things as hard or soft, wet or dry, according to our experience of them.

If you were to touch some fur and then touch some steel, you would notice a difference between them. The fur is soft and the steel is hard. The fur is warm and the steel is cold. But how far are these real differences, integral to the substances, and how far are they differences only in our perception of them?

Fur and steel, if they have been kept in the same room for a while, are both the same temperature. Fur feels warm because it is a thermal insulator. Steel feels cold because it is a conductor of heat – it draws the heat away from our fingers, so we experience it as cold. Fur feels soft because it comprises lots of tiny fibres that can move in the cushion of air between them. We could make fur from steel, but the way we usually experience steel is as a block, not as a steel-and-air mix. (Think about how iron filings feel soft.) Of course, there are also genuine physical differences between materials, which are produced by the arrangement of atoms and molecules.

> 'There is no logical impossibility in the hypothesis that the world sprang into being five minutes ago, exactly as it then was, with a population that "remembered" a wholly unreal past. There is no logically necessary connection between events at different times; therefore nothing that is happening now or will happen in the future can disprove the hypothesis that the world began five minutes ago.'
>
> Bertrand Russell, 1921

IT'S THERE IF WE BELIEVE IT IS

'Consensus reality' is a term for things or situations that are deemed to be real because most people believe they exist. For example, in some modern and many ancient societies, enough people believe in the existence of a God for God's existence to count as consensus reality.

A vehicle travelling over the Moon makes no sound as there is no air to vibrate. Sound needs an interaction of moving thing, air and observer.

John Locke divided the properties of objects into primary and secondary types. The primary properties are belonging to the objects – extension in space, shape, whether the object is moving, and so on. The secondary properties are those which depend on our sensory perceptions of the object, such as colour, weight and the noise it makes. The German philosopher Martin Heidegger believed our understanding of the world is always in relation to ourselves. He described *Dasein*, literally 'being there', as the state of the human. Our existence is defined in terms of our context in the world and it's impossible to separate our individual consciousness from its surrounding environment.

Quantum thereness

One of the most famous icons (perhaps the only famous icon) of quantum physics is Schrödinger's unfortunate cat. In this thought experiment, devised in 1935, Erwin Schrödinger suggested we think of a cat shut in a box (see illustration on facing page). Also in the box is a flask of poison, some radioactive material and a detector measuring radioactivity.

If the detector finds evidence of radioactive decay, the flask is automatically broken and the poison will kill the cat. If there is no radioactive decay, the cat will live.

The state of the cat will not be known until the box is opened. According to quantum theory, the state of the cat is not even *determined* until the box is opened. The cat is simultaneously dead and alive until its state is fixed by observation.

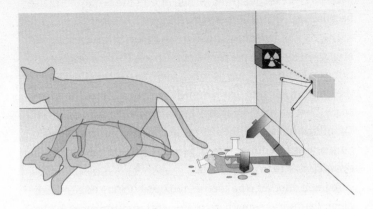

Schrödinger devised the experiment to show how ridiculous some aspects of quantum theory sound when scaled up from the atomic level to the world around us – why is the cat dead *and* alive until its state is *fixed*, rather than dead *or* alive until its state is *known*? The question, as with the tree, is how the presence of an observer impacts on what we think of as reality.

IS THE MOON THERE?

In a (possibly apocryphal) story, Albert Einstein once asked the quantum physicist Niels Bohr if he genuinely believed the Moon only exists when someone is looking at it. Bohr replied that Einstein would not be able to prove it does.

Is nothing something?

'Nothing will come of nothing,' King Lear says to Cordelia. But it would seem that *everything* came from nothing – whether we prefer to see the origins of the universe in God or the Big Bang.

One of the key questions in metaphysics is why there is something rather than nothing (if indeed there is). All something is mostly nothing, and 'nothing' only makes sense because there is something. A void or vacuum is only definable because elsewhere there is something.

There's a lot more nothing than we'd like to think. Each atom is 99.999999999999 per cent empty space. This means that things take up 10^{14} times as much room as they would if all the 'stuff' in an atom was jammed together without the empty space. That's hard to imagine: it means that the Sun, which is 1.4 million km across, would squash down to one-and-a-half hundredths of a millimetre, or 14 microns. That's about a million times denser than a black hole.

To put it another way, there is 100,000,000,000,000 times as much nothing as something in the stuff we think of as matter. And in space there is even less something (or even more nothing). It's the existence of nothing – the space within and between particles – that makes our world possible.

WHY IS THERE SOMETHING RATHER THAN NOTHING?

The existence of the universe is generally accounted for by reference to a 'prime mover' through which everything was created from nothing. There are many myths and religions that have a being as prime mover. Science has the Big Bang as the most likely prime mover of the universe. In both cases, mythical and scientific, the question 'what was before' is meaningless – as meaningless as asking what is north of the North Pole.

What do you know?

How do you know things?
And what can you be sure of?

The acquisition of knowledge has a chequered history. In the Judaeo-Christian tradition, eating the fruit of the Tree of Knowledge led to the fall of man. In medieval legend, Faust sold his soul to the Devil in exchange for an understanding of necromancy and the power it gave him. But without a handy apple or demon, how do most of us gain knowledge?

The blank canvas

A newborn baby acquires a large body of knowledge very quickly. Aristotle was the first to suggest that a baby is born with an empty mind, or 'unscribed tablet' on which experience writes knowledge. Around 1,300 years later, the Persian philosopher Ibn Sina (or Avicenna) used the phrase *tabula rasa* (blank slate): 'human intellect at birth is like a *tabula rasa*, a pure potentiality that is actualized through education, and comes to know.'

The baby has to learn to crawl, then walk, talk, and relate to other people. Neurologists can tell us how the baby's brain grows neurons and connections between them, so it is physically incapable of learning some skills before a particular stage of physical development. But is this evidence that the baby is learning those skills from a position of ignorance?

> 'If we will attentively consider new born children, we shall have little reason to think that they bring many ideas into the world with them . . . [but] by degrees afterward, ideas come into their minds.'
>
> John Locke, 1689

Plato and the knowledgeable soul

Plato thought not. He believed that human souls pre-exist and are allocated to a baby. In their non-incarnated forms, souls have innate knowledge and understanding and can access the realm of forms. Once the soul is housed in a human mind and body, this pure understanding is hidden from it. According to Plato, when we learn, we are uncovering knowledge that is already there, or innate. Not surprisingly, this view is known as innatism. It's as though the soul has been put into a glass cubicle with steamed-up windows and has to wipe them to see what it could previously see clearly when it was outside the cubicle. Even then, it sees through smeary glass rather than seeing things truly. The baby, then, has a lot of knowledge locked in his or her soul, but can't access it without prompting.

Plato sought to demonstrate this by showing how Socrates 'uncovered' knowledge in a slave. At first the slave seems to know nothing of a geometrical formula. By asking questions, Socrates eventually gets the slave to state the formula, thus – he claims – showing that the slave knew it all along but needed help to uncover it. The proof is spurious, of course. Socrates asks questions that direct the slave, through reason, towards the right conclusion.

> '[The soul] is a veritable prisoner bound within his body . . . and that instead of investigating reality by itself and in itself, it is compelled to peer through the bars of its prison.'
>
> Plato

Later innatists suggested that the soul had been provided with a sort of starter-pack of knowledge by God. Ideas which have been postulated as innate include the existence of God (René Descartes), mathematical facts such as $1+1=2$ (Gottfried Leibniz) and ethical truths about right and wrong (Immanuel Kant). If moral knowledge is innate, it must be absolute and unchanging so that which is good or bad is the same for all people in all places and at all times (see Chapter 16). In some cases, people might not be aware of an innate truth, but this is because it hasn't been awakened in them, not because they don't have it. A little nudge or prompt can bring it to the surface.

Rationalists and empiricists

Whether knowledge comes with the soul or must be garnered afresh by each new life, there are two possible principal sources.

We can either gain knowledge through the application of reason or through the evidence of our senses. Those philosophers, like Plato and Descartes, who believed we can arrive at knowledge through the application of reason are called rationalists. Those, like Aristotle and Locke, who believed our senses are the only reliable source of knowledge are called empiricists. Empiricists tend to take the *tabula rasa* view and assume that the infant needs to experience the world in order to learn. Rationalists believe there is innate knowledge, or at least innate structures for arriving at or structuring knowledge.

John Locke

The Scots philosopher David Hume took the empirical view as far as possible and rejected the certainty of everything he could not experience directly himself. This left him denying the existence of God, of all cause and effect, of all knowledge derived by reason and even, ultimately, his own identity. All he could be sure of was that he perceived things. He could not be certain that the perceptions related to anything real. 'I am nothing but a bundle of perceptions,' he concluded.

Can you believe your eyes?

Unless you're colour blind, you probably feel certain of the colour of things. Say you are wearing a red jumper. The property we call 'red' means 'reflects (or emits) red light – electromagnetic radiation with a wavelength of around 650 nanometres'. But although everyone might agree that your jumper is red, I have no way of telling whether I see the same thing as you. We might experience red very differently, but never know it.

Immanuel Kant maintained we can only know the world through our sense perceptions and can't know how the impression we have relates to how – or if – things really are. He pointed out that if we spent our whole lives looking through a distorting lens, we would never know that what we thought we saw was not reality. Interestingly, if people wear glasses that invert the image they see, after a few days their brains adjust to the distortion and they see things the right way up. We see what we expect to see – we can't know how that relates to reality, or if that phrase even has any meaning.

REDSHIFT

It's not just our perception that distorts how reality appears; physics also does it for us. When an object is moving away from you, the wavelength of the light reaching you becomes longer, moving towards the red end of the spectrum. It is a result of the Doppler effect, which causes the noise made by a vehicle speeding past seem to fall and then rise. Redshift makes stars moving away from us as the universe expands look redder than they are – that is, redder than the light they actually emit.

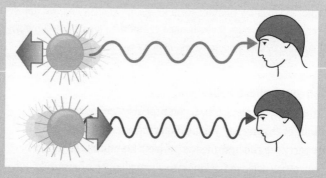

If the star is stationary relative to us, it looks white. If the star is moving away from us, it looks red. If it is moving towards us, it looks blue.

Have faith

Another possible source of knowledge is divine inspiration or being blessed with understanding through faith. St Augustine believed that he could only have full understanding through the grace of God. He put his trust in a line from the Bible: 'unless thou believe thou shalt not understand' (Isaiah 26:3).

Of course, the kind of knowledge that comes with faith is not susceptible to proof. Its reliability will be in doubt for people who don't share the same beliefs as the person who trusts in divine inspiration.

Nativism: hard-wired for knowledge

Immanuel Kant proposed that the infant knows objects in innate ways that don't rely on a trapped knowledge with hazy memories of the realm of forms. Kant's explanation relies on his rather complicated set of 'categories' which describe all objects. More recent accounts of nativism – the idea that we are somehow primed for knowledge – are easier to understand and grounded in something more concrete.

Modern philosophers with an interest in psychology, such as Noam Chomsky and Jerry Fodor, argue that the structure of the brain is primed to accept or structure knowledge in certain ways. It is not that the baby already knows things, but the baby already knows *how* to know things. It's a bit like having a pre-formatted hard drive – it has all the structures set up to accept the data, and it just needs to be filled.

Chomsky points to underlying similarities in linguistic structures to support his argument that language-learning is something the brain is pre-prepared for; but there are other types of knowledge that have to be acquired early on. Children who have since infancy been excluded from human company sometimes never learn to speak, walk upright, eat cooked food or wear clothes. Chomsky feels that the same might be true of moral structures. This idea is supported by the very similar moral values found in different cultures (though it could also be explained by them being the values that make communal life run smoothly).

Chomsky suspects that the structure of the mind might even limit what we can know. Some questions might be beyond us because our brains are not structured in such a way that we can ever understand an answer to them, just as our eyes are not designed to see infrared or our ears to hear very low-frequency sounds. Chomsky thought some questions in philosophy might fall into that category.

NATURE AND NURTURE

The *tabula rasa*/innate knowledge debate is central to the discussion of whether we are made mostly by nature (innate or inherited characteristics) or nurture (the environment and our upbringing). This extends to all areas of social dialogue. Is someone *born* homosexual or do they *become* homosexual? Are some people born with criminal tendencies, or is it the fault of their parents, schooling and social conditioning?

The *tabula rasa* view would say that all that we are comes from nurture. The innatist view would say that it is to a large degree already determined before we are born. Too firm an innatist view can lead to dangerous political policies, including eugenics – the attempt to breed in or out certain characteristics by limiting the gene pool. This is achieved by restrictions on who can have children, and with whom.

CHAPTER 4

When is a biscuit not a biscuit?

How do we go about categorizing the world, and how do we know that the results we come up with are based on reality?

Jaffa Cakes have a spongy base, a blob of orange goo and a coating of chocolate. Does that make them a cake or a biscuit? In 1991, McVities, the manufacturer of Jaffa Cakes, was in dispute with HM Customs and Excise in the UK over just that question. Chocolate-coated biscuits attract VAT (value-added tax), but cakes, whether or not they are iced with chocolate, do not.

How we group things

The human inclination to put things into categories is immense. We classify everything – even, it seems, biscuits and cakes. But does classification reflect divisions in reality or does it create artificial categories?

Aristotle attempted formal categorization more than 2,300 years ago. He believed he was identifying categories that genuinely divided things, a position which makes him a realist. (Someone who believes that categorization is entirely imposed on the classified things is a conceptualist.) Aristotle listed the ten highest categories that could be used to distinguish objects (or possibly words – it's not clear whether he was talking about words or the things words refer to). The ten categories are: **(1) substance** (e.g. man, or horse); **(2) quantity**; **(3) quality** (e.g. white); **(4) relation** (e.g. half, double); **(5) place**; **(6) time**; **(7) being in a position** (e.g. sitting); **(8) having** (e.g. has a hat on); **(9) acting**; and **(10) being acted upon** (e.g. being cut). It's far more complicated than any list suggests. The important distinction is that one thing can't be another – so, for instance, quantity is not a type of substance or a place.

Aristotle has no 'top' category, because to categorize is to draw distinctions and, logically, if everything is in a top category, there is nothing left to be outside it. The categories contain multiple subdivisions, however. We can go up or down through a system of categories to include more or fewer examples. If we had a category of dogs, for instance, we could move more specifically to a category of Dalmatians or more generally to a category of land mammals. The act of categorizing requires investigating things and seeing which are their common features and which distinguish them from other things.

THE CASE FOR AND AGAINST JAFFA 'CAKES'

To decide, the court considered the following points:

- The name includes the word 'cake'.
- Jaffa Cakes are made from an egg, flour and sugar mixture which becomes puffy and aerated on cooking, just like a real cake. The batter is thin, like cake batter, not thick, like biscuit batter.
- Cakes are soft and bendy; biscuits snap. A Jaffa Cake doesn't snap, and has the texture of a sponge cake.
- When it goes stale, a Jaffa Cake goes hard like a cake. When biscuits go stale, they go soft.
- The sponge part of a Jaffa Cake is a substantial part of its bulk.
- Jaffa Cakes are small, like biscuits – a bit too small for a cake.
- Jaffa Cakes are sold in packs that look more like biscuit packets than cake packets.
- Jaffa Cakes are generally displayed for sale with biscuits rather than cakes.
- Jaffa Cakes are presented as a snack to be eaten with the fingers. Cakes are more often eaten with a fork.

The court decided that Jaffa Cakes had enough characteristics of cakes to be accepted as such, and, consequently, they are exempt from VAT.

Being certain – what is necessary and sufficient

To categorize and define adequately, we need to find properties that are necessary and sufficient to put things into one group and not another. Classical categorization provides enough categories for everything to be categorized. The categories must be mutually exclusive – if something is a bird, it can't be a fish; if it is a motorbike, it can't be a car.

Animal or vegetable?

The first large-scale, systematic attempt to categorize living things was made by the Swedish naturalist Carl Linnaeus (see image below) in the 18th century. He worked from visible features to try to establish relationships between organisms, and he developed the familiar division of organisms into kingdom, class, order, genus and species. His *Systema Naturae* was first published in 1735 and was only twelve pages long. The twelfth edition, the last overseen by Linnaeus, was 2,400 pages long and was completed in 1768.

Today, phylogenetics takes a different approach, working from the DNA of organisms to establish 'clades' – groupings dependant on whether organisms share one or more characteristics of the last-known ancestor in their line of evolution.

The intention is to work out how everything that has evolved came from other organisms – a sort of gigantic family tree for the whole of the natural world.

It's not straightforward; often there is more than one way of grouping creatures depending on which features you look at.

Fuzzy tigers

The American philosophers Saul Kripke (born 1940) and Hilary Putnam (born 1926) have attempted to define categories by referring to necessary properties inherent in things – rather like Locke's primary properties (see page 28). If we were trying to define a tiger, we might say that it has stripes and four legs. Although they are the usual features of a tiger, they are not necessary properties, as a tiger might be albino or might have lost a leg and would still be a tiger. To define a tiger more precisely, we could say that it must have tiger DNA. Something that doesn't have tiger DNA can't be a tiger, so tiger DNA is a necessary property. Possessing tiger DNA is not sufficient to identify a tiger, though – the lost leg or a bit of the striped (or albino) fur would have tiger DNA, but could not be called a tiger.

Perhaps we could define a tiger by saying that it is a complete living organism with tiger DNA. But what about a pregnant tiger, about to give birth? It is one autonomous body, but perhaps three or four tigers. There are more microbial cells in the human body than human cells – presumably the same is true of tigers. So there is more not-tiger in a tiger than there is tiger, yet we don't refer to tigers as a colony of microbes inhabiting a structure that has tiger DNA. We are already being selective in how we view things to classify them.

Being uncertain

Boundaries between categories are seldom clear-cut. The English friar William of Ockham, who died in 1347, maintained that all categories – even labels such as 'human' or 'tree' – are just structures we impose on reality in order to help ourselves think about the world. The Austrian philosopher and physicist Ernst Mach (1838–1916) suggested that even the laws of nature or physics that we claim to discover are just the product of our minds, which seek to impose order on our surroundings. The laws are not 'real' – they are simply the best explanation we can come up with in any particular set of circumstances.

There is no biological difference between a flower and a weed. You could say that a 'flower' is a plant that is pleasing to human beings. Is a daisy or dandelion in the lawn a flower or a weed? Is a weed simply a plant in 'the wrong place'?

Who chooses?

Phylogenetics is one way of categorizing living things, and it is a way that is very useful to biologists. But is it intrinsically any more valid than grouping thing by colour, size or ferocity? A scientist would say that the relationships are intrinsic – one type of animal did give rise to another through evolution, and we just need to discover the right relationship.

An artist might group some types of tortoise with some types of cat because they have similar patterns. Perhaps this, too, tells us something useful about the animals. Maybe they both developed this pattern for the same reason (camouflage, for instance). Or perhaps there is something important in beauty. We currently prioritize science, but that doesn't mean science gives a method of categorization that is objectively 'better' or more 'true' than any other.

CHAPTER 5

Tea or coffee?

Do you choose to be the person you are, or is everything about your existence pre-ordained?

Do you believe you are free to choose what you do? Or is everything predestined, right down to whether you will have tea or coffee with your Jaffa Cakes?

Free will and determinism

The belief that everything is predestined, or predetermined, is called determinism. It can come from a religious or spiritual position, or a scientific one. The opposite of determinism is free will – that we are entirely at liberty to act as we choose. Because we don't know what will happen, even if it is predestined, we all feel and act as though we have free will. Indeed, the illusion of free will seems essential. Without it, we would be paralyzed by the knowledge that nothing we do can possibly make any difference to how the future will unfold – we would feel that all action is pointless.

In Ancient Greece and Rome, people appealed to oracles to reveal the future or give them guidance as to how they should act. This suggests they believed the future was mapped out, but not irrevocably so; it was as though there was a strong tendency for certain things to happen, but a person could still intervene to some degree. If people didn't believe this, there would be no point in procuring sacrifices and seeking guidance. We can see a latter-day parallel, perhaps, with the person who learns they have a genetic tendency to heart disease so adopts a healthy lifestyle to minimize the risk.

However, stories such as that of Oedipus – who could not escape killing his father and marrying his mother – show humans reduced to worms wriggling on the hook of fate,

> '*Experience tells us clearly that men believe themselves to be free simply because they are conscious of their actions and unconscious of the causes whereby these actions are determined.*'
>
> Baruch Spinoza, 1632–77

incapable of changing their destiny one jot. What is the use of knowing your destiny if you can't escape it? Oedipus is a tragic and heroic figure because he struggles to do so. We sympathize with his terrible position, and admire the effort he makes to avoid his fate. His response demonstrates greatness of spirit as he tries to do what is right against all the odds. What happens may not be avoidable, but he has power over who he is, and this is manifested in how he behaves.

But is this altogether true? If everything is predetermined, perhaps the futile struggle of Oedipus is too. Or maybe there is a sort of compromise: we are like trains that can't deviate from our track, but we can affect our progress by going quickly or slowly, and we can choose to transport goods or passengers.

Free will to sin?

In the context of a religion which contends that some people will be saved and others damned, the issue of free will is very important. After all, if your destiny is already mapped out for you, what's the point in following the rules? It won't make any difference. Calvinism, a branch of Christianity rooted in the teachings of John Calvin (1509–64), takes that position. It states that the saved/not-saved state of each person is predetermined. This is the doctrine of election. Everyone is born completely sinful and incapable of redemption except through the grace of God. God has already chosen the elect, selected from all eternity, and there is nothing we can do to change our fate.

Being one of the elect is not dependent on the acts or thoughts of the individual, but on criteria known only to God. The same paradox is common to Islam: only those who turn towards Allah will be guided, but Allah chooses who will turn towards him. It would seem that if God has chosen the elect, and they have been chosen for all eternity, we might as well be really self-indulgent – after all, it's not going to make any difference.

For Calvinists, the Holy Spirit 'graciously causes the elect sinner to co-operate, to believe, to repent, to come freely and willingly to Christ'. A tendency to drinking, gambling and lasciviousness is a sign of non-election, so believers keep to the straight and narrow. It's an odd situation – Calvinists follow the rules in order to demonstrate something that has already happened (that God has chosen them for salvation).

Physics and free will

Modern physics holds that physical laws govern everything that happens in the universe, and the laws of physics (probably) don't change over time. This means that right down to the sub-atomic level, every action and reaction is both predictable and inevitable. We can't actually do the predicting a lot of the time, because we have incomplete knowledge and inadequate computing power to do so, but the physical inevitability is still there. Tracing this backwards, everything that has happened since the Big Bang has been inevitable. If we replayed the last 13.8 billion years, exactly the same things would happen again.

In a physicalist universe, we are no more than matter – like all other matter – and our thoughts and intentions are the result of chemical changes in the brain. Everything we think, do and intend must also follow physical laws and be inevitable. This physical determinism robs humankind of free will. We can only reclaim free will through some non-physical animating spirit not subject to scientific laws (see Chapter 6).

Freedom and chaos

Chaos theory studies the dynamics of systems that are sensitive to starting conditions, so that a tiny change at the outset can have a huge effect later on. Although the outcome is governed by physical laws so is theoretically predictable, the conditions and calculations are too complex for predictions to be made. Weather is a good example of a chaotic system: there are so many variables to take into account that an accurate long-range weather forecast is practically impossible even though it is theoretically possible. This has sometimes been illustrated by suggesting that the flapping of a butterfly's wings might cause a storm thousands of kilometres away.

Because chaos theory depends on the effects of changing an initial condition, it assumes that there is, at any point, more than one possible state. The butterfly might or might not flap its

> 'All physical events are caused or determined by the sum total of all previous events.'
>
> Daniel Dennett, 1984

The conceit that the flapping of a butterfly's wings could affect a weather system far away has often been used to explain chaos theory: the idea that everything is part of an incredibly complicated system.

wings – the notion that there is a choice suggests everything is not determined in advance. On the other hand, if all future events are determined by each small choice, where does that leave free will? One answer is to postulate multiple universes – different versions of the universe that exist for all possible choices or events, with new ones branching off at infinite points – whenever you choose tea or coffee, stay in bed late or select one present over another, for instance.

What's your brain doing?

A neurology experiment conducted in the Max Planck Institute in Germany in 2008 has given us new and startling insights into the question of free will. Researchers used an MRI scanner to measure the brain activity of subjects who were choosing whether to press a button with their left or their right hand. By watching the brain's activity, neuroscientists discovered that they could predict the choice the subject was going to make seven seconds before the subject thought they had made a decision. They said this suggests that our sense of choosing is a by-product of subconscious processes. In other words – we don't have free will, but our brains trick us into thinking we do.

As Baruch Spinoza said 350 years ago, 'Men believe themselves to be free simply because they are conscious of their actions and unconscious of the causes whereby these actions are determined.'

Other constraints

If we believe that we are free to act, in that our destinies have not already been irrevocably mapped out by either a deity or the laws of physics, there still remain some constraints.

We can be denied freedom of choice in many ways. A person who is in prison has constrained choices. A person who is paraplegic has constrained choices. A person living in desperate poverty has constrained choices. We can take this idea further and suggest that someone who has not had good opportunities in their youth or access to education has constrained choices, or that someone who is intimidated by a bullying partner or brainwashed by an oppressive regime has constrained choices. At which point, do we say that the forces acting on a person constitute the loss of free will?

If a person is destined to carry out certain acts, whether because of the chemistry of their brain or a divine plan, can we fairly hold them responsible for what they do? Or is choice just an illusion, produced by our brains? Is it acceptable to punish someone for an act that was always going to be inevitable and beyond their control?

Elbow room

Of course, we can't live our lives assuming that we don't have free will. For society to work, we have to cling to the belief that we are free to act. Courts of law assume that people are generally free to act and are responsible for their actions. They don't pause to look into the metaphysical question of whether anyone is free to make a choice. Arguing from historical evidence, we can see that if people see rewards and punishments in place, their behaviour improves. But, of course, it could be that they have always been destined to act like that . . .

Several philosophers have tried to negotiate some space for manoeuvre within the free will/determinism debate. As Dennett points out, if we surrender to determinism we will lurch towards fatalism and despair. A compromise position, called compatibilism, tries to make room for enough free will to let us get by. It depends on people acting freely, but following determined motives – so if you are a generous person, you are free to choose which charity to give to, but you *will* be giving to one of them. As Arthur Schopenhauer put it, 'Man can do what he wills but he cannot will what he wills.' (1839) Others have seen this wiggle room as illusory – or worse: 'a wretched subterfuge' (Immanuel Kant) or a 'quagmire of evasion' (William James).

Too much freedom

The existentialist philosophers of the 20th century took a completely opposite view, giving people more

> *'The destiny of man is placed within himself.'*
> Jean-Paul Sartre, 1946

freedom and responsibility than most of us want. In the words of Jean-Paul Sartre (below), we are 'condemned to be free'.

According to Sartre, our characters are defined by our acts, rather than the other way round. We make ourselves, starting from a clean slate. Sartre didn't argue that we all have the same choices, but contended that those we do have are freely made, even if they are made under duress. We can't say 'I had no choice', because there is always a choice, even if one of the options is unacceptable to us – to die rather than do as a gunman tells us, for instance. Nothing can be blamed on God (who does not exist – though we may choose to believe in him), and nothing may be blamed on any predisposition in our personalities, as we have forged those ourselves through previous decisions we have taken.

To shirk responsibility for our choices is to deceive ourselves.

CHAPTER 6

Is there a ghost in the machine?

What part of you is truly 'you'?

Most world cultures have long believed that the essence of humanity means having a body inhabited by some kind of spirit. It may be a spirit with special religious significance – a fragment of the godhead or of some universal spirit, for instance. Or it may be something closer to a mind, or consciousness, which has no supernatural element. The spirit could be eternal or it might dissipate when the body dies, or even linger in the ether as a ghost. Alternatively there is a possibility that this model could be wrong, and there may be no special animating spirit.

> '*I am present to my body not merely in the way a seaman is present to his ship, but . . . I am tightly joined and, so to speak, mingled together with it, so much so that I make up one single thing with it.*'
>
> René Descartes, *Meditations on First Philosophy* (1641)

Dividing line

Plato believed that the soul, when in a body, was in temporary exile from the realm of forms, trapped and limited in its potential. Similarly for the religious, the soul is often a prisoner in the body, yearning towards goodness or God but dragged down by base impulses to satisfy the body's physical longings. Tension between the two, with the soul always the nobler party, typically characterizes the relationship between them.

Prompted by the increasing interest in mechanics and science of the Enlightenment, René Descartes proposed that the human body is a complex biological machine controlled by a spirit. This theory was later dubbed the 'ghost in the machine'. At first it seems quite intuitive: we know that there is a part of us which thinks, dreams, hopes, experiences, and feels it's separate from the part that breathes or runs upstairs. This separation of ourselves into two parts – the physical and the spiritual or mental – is called dualism. But there are problems with this intuitive separation.

The soul as the prisoner of the body is a familiar image. In this Byzantine mosaic, the incarnate soul is a caged bird.

Mind and body

The body obviously has an impact on the mind or spirit. If we are upset, there is a physical manifestation in tears or changed breathing. If we're injured, we feel pain that might push everything else from our mind. We divide physical movements into conscious and unconscious acts, recognizing a difference between the involuntary action of our heart pumping blood and the chosen action of hugging a child. Although we know which parts of the brain and nervous system are involved in pumping blood or giving a hug, we don't know where to locate the part that makes us want to hug a child.

Descartes thought he had found the spirit in the pineal gland, a small structure buried deep within the brain (see illustration on page 58). He was not the first to do this – the Ancient Chinese called the pineal gland the 'Celestial Eye' and in Hinduism it is the 'window of Brahma'. Still, Descartes wasn't able to explain how the completely non-physical soul could have an effect on the physical body or world. This remains the problem with Cartesian dualism: how can something with no material presence have a physical impact or be affected by the physical?

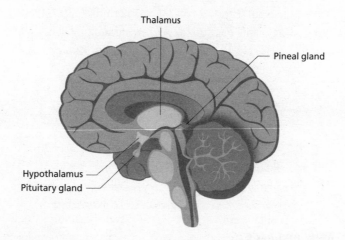

Soulless?

Things are not necessarily true just because they seem sensible or because lots of people believe them (see Chapter 25), so perhaps there isn't really a division between body and soul.

The 20th-century French philosopher Maurice Merleau-Ponty rejected Descartes' body/soul division. Instead he saw the whole human entity as purely biological: 'I am my body.' Bertrand Russell denied the existence of a spirit or soul, saying that the mind comprises simply a collection of mental events – memories, thoughts and experiences.

The British philosopher Gilbert Ryle (1900–76) argued that our sense of a division between mind and body comes about because of the way we use language to describe the physical and spiritual separately.

The American philosopher Daniel Dennett argues that all aspects of character, thought, personality and consciousness are effects of neurology, entirely determined and created by the biochemistry of the brain and body. If nothing distinguishes the mind from the body, it suggests there is nothing special about humans to distinguish them from other animals. Dennett goes further, and says there is nothing special about living beings at all – a computer that *seems* intelligent *is* intelligent. He sees a ghost in a literal machine (though it is not a ghost, but an artefact).

Brains are conscious like water is wet

The American philosopher John Searle sees consciousness as an 'emergent property' – something that develops when enough neurons get together. An emergent property is something that can only be detected when a lot of something is together. The wetness of water is an emergent property – a single molecule of water is not wet, but water *en masse* is wet. Similarly a single neuron is probably not conscious, but a group of them produces consciousness. Searle considers consciousness as entirely a physical effect, produced by the neurochemistry of the brain, and not remotely mystical or 'other'.

Where does it start?

Whether we take a neurological or a spiritual view of the conscious, thinking part of being human, there is a question of where it comes from and when it starts. For many religions, mythology accounts for this, with the soul entering the body at or at some point before birth.

Humans, as we know, attain a high level of consciousness; so when in the development of the individual does the soul emerge? This is a more pressing question than it might at first appear, since any theoretical answer should inform our views on how the pre-born are treated, including testing, medical procedures and, most obviously, abortion.

Three weeks after the fertilization of the human egg, the embryo's brain and spinal cord begin to develop. This is the point at which, if consciousness is an emergent property of neural activity, the new human could begin to be conscious. Babies born at around 22 weeks of gestation occasionally survive, so perhaps that sets an upper limit on the development of consciousness.

It's not just the development of the individual human that poses a difficult question. If a spirit or consciousness is not human and special, when in evolution might it spring into being? How many neurons have to be present for consciousness to start? We might assume that there are gradations of consciousness. Perhaps other mammals can feel pleasure or anticipation? But few people imagine, say, impala or alligators pondering the nature of evil, wondering whether there is an afterlife, or developing differential calculus (not that we have any evidence that they don't, of course – see Chapter 13).

HAVING A SOUL CAN SAVE YOUR LIFE

In many societies, consciousness brings with it entitlements and responsibilities. In medical care, evidence of consciousness in a patient is sufficient reason to keep him or her alive with artificial help. In some jurisdictions, people who commit crimes while asleep are not considered responsible for their actions.

In the past, madness was seen as a disorder of the soul or the presence of a demon. The opposite of this – when the soul's powerful presence produces religious frenzy – was deemed very special (though was sometimes misunderstood). Current legal practice allows a claim of diminished responsibility if mental illness clouds a person's judgement.

CHAPTER 7

Who do you think you are?

Are you defined by your genes, or your job? Is there even any stable thing that is identity?

'You're not the man/woman I married' has long been the cry of a partner in a failing marriage. 'He's not half the man he used to be,' is sometimes said of a person who's wasted by illness or experiencing a middle-aged decline. Are we who we were? And who were we anyway, whenever 'were' happened? What is the thing we call 'I'?

Bones and boats

The human body is made up of cells of different types. These don't last the 80–100 years you might hope them to – they wear out and are replaced, some of them very frequently. In fact, you lose millions of cells every second. The cells lining your gut take a real battering as they're bathed in acid and bombarded by semi-digested food all the time: a colon cell lasts only about four days. Cells on the outside of the gut, away from all that acid, can last up to 16 years. And there are a few cells which, once they're gone, are gone for good. Neurons in most areas of the brain are never replaced, so it's not a good idea to kill them off on drinking binges. But these are rare exceptions – very, very little of you is the 'you' that you were at birth.

The 1st-century Greek historian and essayist Plutarch tackled the issue of change and permanence through the paradox of Theseus's ship. As parts of the ship wore out, they were replaced with identical new parts. If the mast broke, a new mast was fitted. If the sails tore, new sails were stitched, and so on. Eventually none of the original parts remained. Was it still the same ship? If someone had made a second ship using all the replacement parts, but while the first ship was new and functional, we would never consider that the second ship was the same as the first (co-existing) ship. Two things can't be the same thing. Somehow, the slow replacement of the components makes the question meaningful. If the repaired ship is not the same ship as the original, at what point did it stop being the same?

Mind and time

We don't usually think of ourselves as just a collection of body tissues made up of cells. Most of us consider our identity to be something nebulous, spiritual, to do with consciousness or even a soul (see Chapter 6) – something that is the 'self'.

The English philosopher John Locke (1632–1704) located identity entirely in the thinking mind, which endures through time and is aware of itself. He believed that the mind of the newborn child was a *tabula rasa*, or blank slate, upon which identity and knowledge were written by experience as the child developed (see Chapter 3).

This seems to make sense because we can conceive of still existing as the same 'self' even if we were to have a horrible accident and somehow survive as only a brain (or mind) in an entirely prosthetic body. But the Scottish philosopher Thomas Reid (1710–96) found Locke's account too simplistic. If our identity is rooted in past experience, he argued, what happens when we forget that past experience? Reid devised the 'brave officer' argument to demonstrate his point:

> '*[The self is] that conscious thinking thing, (whatever substance, made up of whether spiritual, or material, simple, or compounded, it matters not) which is sensible, or conscious of pleasure and pain, capable of happiness or misery, and so is concerned for itself, as far as that consciousness extends.*'
>
> John Locke, 1689

'Suppose a brave officer to have been flogged when a boy at school for robbing an orchard, to have taken a standard from the enemy in his first campaign, and to have been made a general in advanced life; suppose, also, which must be admitted to be possible, that, when he took the standard, he was conscious of his having been flogged at school, and that, when made a general, he was conscious of his taking the standard, but had absolutely lost the consciousness of his flogging.'

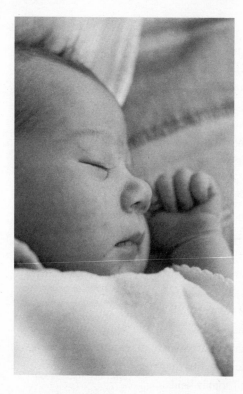

The idea of the infant's mind as a blank slate on which education and identity would later be written can be traced back to Aristotle.

According to Locke, the general must be the same person as the brave officer, and the brave officer must be the same person as the boy, as the boy and the officer are linked by continuity of consciousness, as are the officer and the general. But as there is no psychological connection between the general and the boy, they are not the same person. Reid's argument shows the contradiction inherent in Locke's definition, because the general both is and is not the same person as the boy who was flogged at school.

The existentialist philosophers of the 20th century saw the self as a work in progress, constantly defined and redefined by its actions. This echoes the psychological theory that personality is influenced by past experiences, including some we have forgotten. But, unlike psychologists, the existentialists

rejected any suggestion that we can hold our genetic make-up
or past experiences to account for who we turn out to be. Sartre
maintained that most people had got it the wrong way round: we
don't act 'in character' but act 'to make' our characters. If you act
in a selfish way, you are a selfish person – but you can redefine
yourself by acting unselfishly tomorrow. There is no need for
continuity of consciousness; character is cumulative, built in the
chain of actions that brought you to the present moment.

Being rid of the self

We have seen that for many philosophers there is a need to
locate identity somewhere apart from the body. But for the
Scots philosopher David Hume, the self is nothing but a bundle
of perceptions – it has no unity, nor really even any existence.
The whole concept of self was, to him, a fiction. Even the word
'bundle' suggests some oneness, some collecting together. It
seems that it's impossible to talk about human beings and
eradicate the self from the language we use. For Hume, the self
was a sort of commonwealth of experiences, bits and pieces

constantly coming in and out – like Theseus's ship, but in a non-physical form. Daniel Dennett agrees with Hume that the body and its perceptions are all we have. For him, the self exists in the neural connections of the brain and nothing else – it's just a convenience that helps us to talk about ourselves.

Some Eastern philosophies see the self as an erroneous perception produced by the body and masking the reality that we are part of a larger whole. The existence of the self is, in these traditions, an illusion, and one we are best rid of as quickly as possible since it stands in the way of enlightenment.

CHAPTER 8

Bad things happen – but why?

Why is life full of pain and misery?
Is the universe unfathomable or
simply indifferent?

In our lives we may encounter misfortune and, occasionally, truly terrible events. A natural response to overwhelming misfortune is to ask 'why me?' or 'why did this have to happen?' This is the thin end of the wedge. The thick end of the wedge is 'why does *anything* happen?', but people rarely pause to ask why good things happen.

In philosophical circles, 'why bad things happen' is part of 'the problem of evil', one of the most compelling arguments against the existence of God. The basics were laid out by Epicurus in the 3rd century BC, who asked: 'Is God willing to prevent evil, but not able? Then he is not omnipotent. Is he able, but not willing? Then he is malevolent. Is he both able and willing? Then how can there be evil?'

Why? vs. Why not?

There are, broadly speaking, two possible answers to the question: why do bad things happen?

- They happen because of a greater purpose

- They happen for no reason.

The first answer needs something or someone 'out there' setting the purpose. Let's call that purposeful something God – a supreme, all-powerful being. The second answer is harder to process. If life goes well, you can get by knowing that bad things happen for no reason; otherwise you might drift down the futility spiral, feeling powerless and terrified.

The greater purpose

Central to many religions is the belief that a controlling deity has some Grand Plan which, if we could only glimpse it, would explain why everything happens. Religions tend to suggest a

God who is good – there wouldn't be much solace in an evil God. But why would a God who is good allow bad things to happen?

If God is benevolent, it suggests that there is a silver lining lurking inside even the greyest cloud, or that the things we consider to be bad are perhaps not really bad – they just seem so because we aren't seeing the bigger picture which makes everything clear. Or perhaps God is using adversity to test us and/or give us a chance for spiritual growth. (You might regard this as a kind of silver lining.)

The Ministry of Truth version – bad is good

In George Orwell's novel *Nineteen Eighty-Four* (published in 1949), the totalitarian state has a Ministry of Truth which defines what is 'true' and what is not. 'Bad is good' could well be one of its slogans. St Augustine argued that God brings good out of evil: 'Since God is the highest good, He would not allow any evil to exist in His works, unless His omnipotence and goodness were such as to bring good even out of evil.'

This is not a robust philosophical argument because it starts with the assumption that God 'would not allow any evil to exist' and uses it to justify the idea that evil therefore isn't really evil. If we could just see things from God's point of view, it would be clear to us that the bad things are not really bad, but part of a larger good. Unfortunately we can't see things from God's point of view so we have to take it on trust, which can be hard to do.

Occasionally, well-meaning friends will make remarks such as 'we're not sent more than we can bear' in response to hearing about someone's misfortunes. (This so clearly and patently untrue it's astonishing that anyone ever says it.) It's based on the notion that someone or something is setting tests and trials, perhaps to strengthen us.

The British cleric and political theorist Thomas Malthus (1766–1834) believed that evil existed as a spur to action, prompting us to find ways to avoid or correct it: 'Evil exists in the world not to create despair, but activity.'

God's not looking

Of course, there might be a God with a grand scheme but no interest in individual humans. The scheme might involve, for example, creating a race of beings who are used for experimental purposes. Just as biologists breed strains of fruit flies to experiment in genetics, they could breed people as part of some cosmic science experiment. In this case, there would be no particular purpose to the suffering of individuals or groups – it would just be something that emerges or is inflicted during the course of the experiment.

Alternatively, God might not want to intervene in human affairs or might not be able to do so. It's possible that God set the universe working, but now it just runs itself. This view of God as something like a divine watchmaker was proposed by Isaac Newton and others. If the world runs automatically following its laws, bad things happen because they are the consequences of other things that have happened, or because of a design flaw; there is no determined and specific purpose. The situation is much the same as if there were no God at all.

Another possibility suggested by those who have been disillusioned by events, but still cling to the idea of a God, is that God is either indifferent to the fates of humans or is actively malevolent. There is no good reason why this shouldn't be true because a malevolent god is just as likely to exist as a benevolent one.

As few bad things happen as possible

In 1710, Gottfried Leibniz proposed a view known as optimism. In philosophical terms, optimism doesn't mean believing that each half-empty glass is half full; it means optimalism – that everything is as good as it can be. God has created the optimal world – the best world from all the many possible worlds he could have created. It's as though God has his hands tied. He'd like to create a world with no evil, no hunger and no malaria-carrying mosquitoes, but for one reason or another, he can't. So we've got the world as it is. And we can rest assured that it couldn't be any better than this.

This view was satirized by Voltaire in his novella *Candide*. It's easy to see how small evils or inconveniences might be the best alternative of a bad lot. But it's hard to look back in history and imagine what might have been worse alternatives to events such as the Holocaust or the Black Death.

It's all your fault

Some Eastern religions propose that we are reborn over and over again, with souls that are struggling towards enlightenment

THE BEST OF ALL POSSIBLE WORLDS?

In Voltaire's satirical tale, the young Candide is taught by his optimistic and philosophically inclined tutor, Pangloss, that 'all is for the best in this best of all possible worlds.' Candide goes on to suffer terrible hardships and cruelties, which cause him to question his tutor's wisdom. He survives his trials and eventually achieves peace of mind in a simple life untrammelled by notions of idealism. Voltaire's caustic commentary on the social ills of his day demonstrates the danger of slavishly following the philosophical beliefs of others.

(see Chapter 13). Some of the things that happen to you in this life are the consequence of your behaviour in previous incarnations. As you can't remember the previous incarnations, the punishment is completely dissociated from the crime.

There is no reason

Democritus, writing in the 4th and 5th centuries BC, said everything that happens is brought about by the behaviour of atoms. This extraordinarily modern idea is borne out by quantum physics, which says that because everything in the universe follows the laws of physics, which have been and always will be the same, everything would be predictable if only we had the knowledge to predict it. The bad and good things that happen are therefore inevitable (see Chapter 5). Physical inevitability isn't a purpose, it is an account of why things happen.

If everything is not inevitable, and there is no controlling deity, and you aren't having to atone for things you did in a previous incarnation, you are left with the unsettling conclusion that things happen just because they do. There is no controlling fate, no overarching justice, the world doesn't care what happens to us. Life isn't fair – and it's illogical of us to expect it to be.

CHAPTER 9

What goes around comes around – or does it?

Does good (or bad) rebound on those who do good (or bad) themselves?

When someone is unkind to you it's comforting to think that 'what goes around, comes around'; in other words, bad things will happen to those who have slighted or spited us. But is there any substance to this belief?

The concept of karma

Karma has its origins in Hinduism. Its literal meaning is 'act' or 'deed', but it also relates to a system of actions and consequences. The general principle of karma is that if we do good deeds, we will enjoy good fortune and if we do bad deeds, we will suffer. It's a diffuse doctrine of cause and effect, which instead of relating one action directly to its effects has general goodness and badness spread out over time. A similar idea in the Christian faith is: 'as ye sow, so shall ye reap' (Galatians, 6:7).

In this carving from a Jain temple in Ranakpur, India, the knots represent the interlinking laws of karma.

In line with Hindu beliefs about reincarnation, karma refers to your previous incarnations as well as your actions as a human in your current incarnation. The idea is that if you've been generally quite good – as you live now, and perhaps previously as a snail, panda, jellyfish or whatever – you will reap the rewards by having a fairly good time. The useful get-out is that if you are really good as a human being in the here and now, but you're suffering a terrible run of bad luck, it could be retribution for your dreadful behaviour as a previous human, snail, panda or jellyfish.

There are different versions of karma. Some religions, including Hinduism, have a deity meting out karma; others make it a secular cause-and-effect doctrine. Bad karma is a black substance which builds up in other dimensions as we live repeated lives. Only by working off our bad karma can we become enlightened. As being ill uses up bad karma, some believers don't take medicines. In Jainism, bad karma can be produced simply by thinking evil thoughts – they don't even have to be put into action.

Don't rock the boat

The 19th-century German philosopher Friedrich Nietzsche would have considered a belief in karma to be a 'slave religion' because it keeps people subjugated. If they act well, they can expect a reward later; if bad things happen to them, they brought it on themselves in a previous life. There is no incentive to strive to be better treated (ill treatment is even a godsend as it helps to work off the bad karma), and there is every incentive to be obedient, compliant and good.

Other religions take the view that suffering in the present will be rewarded by bliss after death, and that those who enjoy worldly pleasures now will pay dearly for them in the afterlife. It's a similar *quid pro quo* system, but – as with reincarnation – the consequences are substantially separated from the deed and are not verifiable.

Quick turn-around

In folk wisdom, 'what goes around, comes around' has developed a much more focused and short-term meaning: if we behave well towards others, we will in turn be treated well, and if we behave badly towards others, we'll come to grief sooner or later. It can be a comforting thought, and there is no doubt some truth in it. Those who persistently mistreat others are more likely to receive unsympathetic treatment because we are nicer to those who are nice to us. But it's not universally true. We all know people who have behaved badly to a string of partners and still manage to find another, or workplace bullies who get ahead and even have friends, somehow.

We cling to the idea of fairness even when we don't find it manifested in the world. When we are suffering, 'fairness' seems to consist either in others also suffering or in ourselves enjoying better fortune later, so we try to rationalize those desires.

The Wheel of Fortune

In his *Consolation of Philosophy*, 5th-century Roman philosopher Boethius described the random nature of events by showing the allegorical figure of Fortune (always a woman) turning a giant wheel, like a fairground Ferris wheel, to which humans are strapped. Sometimes people are at the top (enjoying good fortune), but there will inevitably come a fall into misfortune – 'what goes up, must come down'. The capriciousness of Fortune became a popular trope in the Middle Ages,

> '**Philosophers say that Fortune is insane and blind and stupid, and they teach that she stands on a rolling, spherical rock: they affirm that, wherever chance pushes that rock, Fortune falls in that direction. They repeat that she is blind for this reason: that she does not see where she's heading; they say she's insane, because she is cruel, flaky and unstable; stupid, because she can't distinguish between the worthy and the unworthy.'**
>
> Pacuvius, 220–130BC

although it's first found in Rome in the 2nd century BC.

Fortune's Wheel does not reward or punish people according to their prior conduct. Instead Fortune is capricious in her elevation and destruction of people – except that the pattern of a turning wheel means those who are at the top will always fall down and those at the bottom will always rise. And Fortune can spin the wheel as quickly or slowly as she likes.

> 'Fortune is ever most friendly and alluring to those whom she strives to deceive, until she overwhelms them with grief beyond bearing, by deserting them when least expected. . . . Are you trying to stay the force of her turning wheel? Ah! dull-witted mortal, if Fortune begin to stay still, she is no longer Fortune.'
>
> Boethius, AD524

Who turns the wheel?

Anyone who believes in an interventionist God can be reassured by the idea that someone is doling out the rewards and punishments required by karma. For those who don't believe that God takes an interest, there is just the cause-and-effect mechanism to punish those who behave badly and reward those who act well; or there is a kind of spiritual balancing act along the lines of the original Hindu karma, best thought of in terms of the water cycle – perpetual, natural and uninterested in its impact on individuals.

Alternatively we can take the view that there is no pattern. Outside the limited arena of human interactions, there is little in terms of cause and effect. There are reckless or cautious acts which can affect our chances of good or bad outcomes, but no one can guarantee their own fortune. You may develop cancer, have an accident or lose a loved one at any point in your life and through no fault of your own. You can suffer all of those events in a year – or never. Similarly you could fall in love, win the lottery and be nominated for a Nobel prize all in the same year.

IT'S ABSURD

The philosophical notion of absurdism relates to the human search for meaning in the face of an ultimately meaningless universe. It began with the work of Swedish philosopher Søren Kierkegaard and French existentialist Albert Camus (below). Taking a position entirely contrary to that of karma or Fortune's Wheel, it allows no pattern in what happens to us beyond physical cause and effect. So, if you are generous to old people and kind to your neighbours, you're just as likely to get cancer or fall off a cliff as if you stole from the elderly and blew up your neighbours' house. Why, then, should you be a good person? Perhaps because it might make you feel happy in yourself?

CHAPTER 10

Will a new iPhone make you happy?

Can happiness be found in buying things? Is it possible to be truly happy?

What makes you happy? Buying luxuries such as an expensive car? Lying on a beach with a cocktail? Playing music? Helping other people? The pursuit of happiness is a perennial human goal. But what truly makes us happy, and how can we achieve it?

We need to be clear about what we mean by happiness. In philosophy, happiness can mean well-being, a life that is well-lived (in the view of the one living it) or it can be a state of mind.

FIRST, DEFINE 'HAPPY'

Abigail works for a disaster charity. She spends her days helping to piece back together the lives of people who have lost everything. She lives in poor conditions and often goes to bed exhausted and traumatized by what she has seen. But her work saves lives. She considers she is living well and would not change what she does.

Joan likes to watch reality TV shows. She lies on the sofa, watching TV and eating doughnuts, which are her favourite food. She has enough money to do this as often as she likes. She is never hungry and never has to work; she never thinks about the hardships other people suffer and goes to bed content each night.

Which of them is happy? Which has a good life?

Reasons to be cheerful . . .

When people ask how they can become happy, they don't generally mean they want a quick burst of bliss; they want to know how to live a life that is satisfying and/or fits their idea of living well. It's quite subjective as we all have different ideas of what 'living well' would be. A life that is full of pleasure is not necessarily the same as a life well lived. There are at least three routes to happiness: the hedonistic way involves having lots of pleasurable experiences; the life-satisfaction way involves being satisfied with how your life is going; the emotional-state way involves feeling affirmed or flourishing emotionally.

Wine, women and song

The hedonistic view finds happiness in pleasurable experiences. We find it first set out in the teachings of Aristippus of Cyrene (c.435–c.356BC). The Cyrenaics considered pleasure to be the only good, and their way was to indulge in every available pleasure, whenever possible. They did bring in some measure of judgement, deeming that some pleasures lead almost immediately to pain, which is to be avoided. Even a Cyrenaic wouldn't have jumped off a high building for the fleeting pleasure of flying. On the whole, though, they valued physical pleasures above mental or spiritual pleasures, so if you fancied a wild night out in Ancient Greece, Aristippus was your man.

Epicurus (341–270BC) took a more measured view. He promoted the virtues of good food, wine, music and other sensual pleasures as a source of happiness, but warned that indulgence should not be indiscriminate or all-out hedonistic. His name has come down to us in the adjective 'Epicurean' to denote someone who enjoys fine dining and good living. Unlike a Cyrenaic, an Epicurean has taste and refinement. Epicurus found pleasure in moderation. His personal tastes were quite modest: he drank water, ate mostly home-grown vegetables, and lived in a sort of commune with friends. This afforded them all plenty of intelligent and sympathetic conversation, and freed them from having to do unpleasant work for people they didn't like in Athens – a bit of a hippie idyll, really.

Epicurus thought seriously about happiness. Once basic physical needs for food, shelter and health had been met, he considered the basic 'goods' necessary to happiness were friendship, freedom and thought (intellectual stimulation and conversation). He considered it natural but unnecessary to desire fancy food, a nice house and the trappings of wealth. He considered it unnatural to want power and fame. So winning *The X-Factor* wouldn't have made him happy.

Find out what you want

Another way of looking at happiness is the satisfaction of desires. That's not the same as having pleasurable experiences, although it can involve them. If you

are constantly frustrated because you can't find a job you enjoy or don't have the relationship you want, you are unlikely to be happy. You might have fleeting periods of happiness produced by hedonistic experiences, but your overall dissatisfaction will mean that you don't consider yourself to be generally happy. We don't all want the same things, so one person might be satisfied with a

ABOUT THAT IPHONE . . .

How would your life be better if you had an iPhone? How would it be worse if you didn't have one? Do you want an iPhone so that you can communicate with friends and use its features? Or do you want one because everyone is supposed to want one and you'll look cool if you have one? Writing in the 1st century BC, Lucretius complained that what people want is dictated by popular opinion rather than their own judgement. And he didn't even have an iPhone.

life that another would hate. To know whether you are satisfied, you have to know what you desire.

The happiness wish-list

There is another model of happiness which philosophers call the 'objective list' model. This is less personal, as it sets out the things that philosophers believe are necessary for well-being, or a good life, in all people. Epicurus' list of friends, freedom and thought is an example. He supposed that possession of these would make a good life for anyone. Aristotle believed that all things yearn to fulfil their function or do what they are best suited to doing.

We might see this as realizing our personal potential. For him, what humans were good at – their function – was rational thought, so people are happiest (or they 'live well') when they live a virtuous life of reason.

Epicurus believed that people who think they enjoy things which are bad for them – drinking too much, being lazy and so on – are not truly happy. Another option, for those people who weren't capable of rational thinking, was to live a life of moral virtue. Aristotle believed that happiness was the only thing we desired for its own sake. We might want other things, such as wealth, friendship and health, but we only want them because we believe they will make us happy.

DOES MONEY MAKE YOU HAPPY?

It's tempting to think you'd be happier with more money so that you could buy the things you want, do what you like, work less and worry less. But various studies have shown it's not that simple. Up to a certain point, increasing income does correspond to increasing reported happiness, but after that point it doesn't make a difference. The point is not particularly high – one study put it at $73,000 a year (£45,000), another at $161,000 (£100,000) a year. It's sufficient to meet basic needs and remove anxiety, but happiness does not appear to increase with excess wealth – having the money to buy yachts and private planes, for example. In a depressing reflection of human nature, it appears that having more money than others makes us happier. but dreaming of a lottery win is not the answer. People who suddenly become richer may feel happier in the short term but soon settle back to their previous level.

Happiness hereafter

For the religious, even if things are not so good now, there is always the promise of everlasting bliss after death. This can be a comfort in difficult times, but it's not the same as happiness. According to St Thomas Aquinas, only imperfect happiness is possible on Earth, and the best form of this comes from the contemplative life – spiritual reflection and worship. We can't all manage that, at least not all the time, so there's a slightly less good option which is to live an active but good life – a life of virtue that is useful to others and pleasing to God.

Is avoiding unhappiness the same thing as being happy? In times when life is very harsh it might seem the best to hope for. Some Eastern religions and philosophies promote a detachment which encourages us to take a step back, observe and acknowledge what happens and how we feel about it, but not let ourselves be ruled by events and feelings.

The Stoics of Ancient Greece took the same view – we can't stop ourselves feeling pain or disappointment but we can limit its impact on our equilibrium. In modern parlance, this is akin to mindfulness. But if it helps to reduce the impact of negative events and feelings, it must also reduce the impact of positive effects and feelings. Perhaps whether or not you opt for a mindful approach depends on whether you expect good things or bad things to come your way.

St Thomas Aquinas said: 'There is within every soul a thirst for happiness and meaning'.

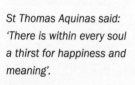

Virtue makes you happy

We've seen that Aristotle saw virtuous living as the path to happiness – but 'virtue' is a vague term. Aristotle visualized a spectrum for all types of behaviour, with vice lying at the extremes at each end of the spectrum and virtue lying in the middle at the point of moderation. The virtue of courage lies between cowardice and recklessness. Generosity is the favoured point between miserliness and profligacy. It's a view that plenty of philosophers have shared.

If we live virtuously, the theory goes, we will be protected to some extent from the vicissitudes of fortune. It's not that misfortune won't touch us, it's that our source of security and contentment lies within ourselves, so is sheltered from fortune's worst effects. The German philosopher Arthur Schopenhauer doubted human happiness was possible, but said if it was then it was the point of life. He believed that three things contribute to human happiness: what you are, what you have and what others think of you. The first is most important, but the second two are what most people are more concerned with. They notice, too late, that what you have and what others think of you aren't so important after all.

> '[Virtue is] a firm and constant will to bring about everything we judge to be the best and to employ all the force of our intellect in judging well . . .
> [it is] the only good, among all those we can possess, which depends entirely on our free will.

> '[Happiness is] perfect contentment of mind and inner satisfaction . . . which is acquired by the wise without fortune's favour. . . . We cannot ever practice any virtue – that is to say, do what our reason tells us we should do – without receiving satisfaction and pleasure from doing so.'
>
> René Descartes, 1645

Glass half-full or glass half-empty?

The standard definition of an optimist is someone who considers a glass half-full; a pessimist considers the same glass half-empty. This basic approach can make a huge difference to your level of happiness and to how you experience life. A pessimist is often cautious and risk-avoidant, expecting things not to work out. An optimist, who takes risks expecting a good outcome, is more likely to encounter the ups and downs of success and disappointment. Some people are happier with a calm life, others yearn for a life of excitement; either way can lead to happiness.

CHAPTER 11

Would you want to live forever?

We spend our lives seeking to avoid death, but would life without end be an even worse prospect?

Most cultures have stories of 'eternals' – humans who can live forever – vampires, for example. But would everlasting life really be a good idea?

What good is death?

Religious and spiritual advisers usually recommend calm acceptance or resignation in the face of death, and spiritual preparation for a 'good death'. Why? Some elderly people, certainly, are ready for death. But many people – especially younger people facing death – are not, and raging 'against the dying of the light', as Dylan Thomas advised, is the natural reaction. We rage against it because we still have things to do, people to love, words to say; because we don't want to have run out of time.

In 1927, the German philosopher Martin Heidegger wrote about the awareness of mortality that presses down on human consciousness. He wrote of 'Dasein' – literally 'being there' – as the state of the individual in the world. We are, he said, defined and limited by our context in time and space. One aspect of that context is that we live for a limited time. Knowing that we only have a limited lifespan causes anxiety (*angst*) or dread. Heidegger didn't believe in a God, but even if he had, God is irrelevant in this scheme. We still have to choose how to spend our time on Earth, and to make that choice wisely as there is no second chance. Death concentrates the mind wonderfully.

'This is, if you like, our curse. It's the price we pay for being so damned clever. We have to live in the knowledge that the worst thing that can possibly happen, one day surely will. . . . We each live in the shadow of a personal apocalypse.'

'[Running from death] is the foundation of human achievement: it is the wellspring of religion, the muse of philosophy, the architect of our cities, and the impulse behind the arts.'

Stephen Cave, British philosopher, 2012

The awareness of our mortality forces us to decide what is important and to focus on it. Heidegger distinguished between authentic and

> 'But at my back I always hear
> Time's winged chariot hurrying near;
> And yonder all before us lie
> Deserts of vast eternity.'
>
> Andrew Marvell (1621–78),
> 'To His Coy Mistress'

inauthentic ways of living. The authentic version was a life lived according to our own values and choices. We could allow ourselves to be pushed about by circumstances, and that would be an inauthentic life, though as we would have chosen the path of least resistance, that too is a sort of authenticity. If, like the vampire, we had all of eternity to fulfil our ambitions, they wouldn't really be ambitions. Nothing would be meaningful as it wouldn't be chosen over anything else – there would be time enough for everything. It is the certain knowledge of death that gives life meaning.

The message we don't want to hear

The quest to live forever, or at least a bit longer, is probably as old as humanity. For thousands of years, magicians and scientists have sought an elixir that will restore youth or let us live forever. Today we have creams, pills and supplements that promise to stop the clock and keep us looking and feeling young. For the very wealthy, cryogenics also offers a way, supposedly, of preserving ourselves for future resuscitation. .

Many religions offer a promise of eternal life after death. In the past, the promise of a better time in the afterlife was probably more compelling than it is now. When most people endured a short life filled with pain and hard work, the idea of an afterlife in which all their suffering would be alleviated must have been very appealing. Today, although many of us

> 'Tomorrow,' said Toad. 'I will do it all tomorrow.'
>
> Arnold Lobel, Days with Frog and Toad, 1979

live much more comfortably and for a lot longer, the promise of eternal life still eludes us. Instead we hope to live on through our children, or through leaving a body of work that will endure into the future.

Some people pay huge sums of money to have their bodies or even just their brains frozen after death. The idea is that when there is a cure for whatever killed them they will be defrosted and able to carry on living. Would you want to live in a new world, long after all your loved ones had died? And why would people of the future want to defrost anyone from the 21st century?

What good is life?

'All the labour of the ages,' said Bertrand Russell, 'all the devotion, all the inspiration, all the noonday brightness of human genius, are destined to extinction in the vast death of the solar system, and the whole temple of man's achievement must inevitably be buried beneath the debris of a universe in ruins.' It's said that Bertrand Russell was once asked by a London cab driver 'what's it all about, then?' He possibly wasn't the best person to ask. But if we are going to die and it's all turning to dust, what use is life? This is the question that the absurdists faced (see Chapter 27).

> 'The mystery of human existence lies not in just staying alive, but in finding something to live for.'
>
> Fyodor Dostoyevsky, 1880

There are two ways to approach the question of the purpose of life. One is to ask whether life needs a purpose. The other is to try to name a purpose. We could go through all the possible purposes of life, but most philosophers come, one way or another, to say that we can't know if it has a purpose so let's just live it the best way we can. Camus, who said the only truly significant question in philosophy is 'why not suicide?', hit the nail on the head when he said that we really just have to get on with it without knowing why we should do so.

> 'Death is not an event in life: we do not live to experience death. If we take eternity to mean not infinite temporal duration but timelessness, then eternal life belongs to those who live in the present. Our life has no end in the way in which our visual field has no limits.'
>
> Ludwig Wittgenstein, 1921

> 'The clear awareness of having been born into a losing struggle need not lead one into despair. I do not especially like the idea that one day I shall be tapped on the shoulder and informed, not that the party is over but that it is most assuredly going on – only henceforth in my absence. (It's the second of those thoughts: the edition of the newspaper that will come out on the day after I have gone, that is the more distressing.) Much more horrible, though, would be the announcement that the party was continuing forever, and that I was forbidden to leave. Whether it was a hellishly bad party or a party that was perfectly heavenly in every respect, the moment that it became eternal and compulsory would be the precise moment that it began to pall.'
>
> Christopher Hitchens, 1949–2011

If you feel there is a purpose to your life (perhaps through religious belief), you won't be asking the question. If you don't, you might take the most frequently given philosophical answer – to live true to yourself, to live a good life, and to do what is right (see Chapter 10). The 'good' of something is what we make of it.

CHAPTER 12

Can you choose to believe in God?

Can you choose your faith, or does it choose you? If belief is not a choice, why should we reward it?

When we pose the question 'Does God exist?', our reason says 'No', but faith may say 'Yes'. The critical question is whether you can *choose* faith.

Pascal's wager

One of the more famous philosophical propositions is Pascal's wager. Faced with uncertainty about whether God exists, Pascal weighed up the costs and benefits of believing or not believing:

- If God does not exist, but we choose to believe in him, we live a virtuous life, lose a little time in fruitless prayer, and disappear into oblivion on death.
- If God does exist, but we choose not to believe in him, we can have a riotous time for a few years, but then lose our immortal souls to an eternity of perdition and torment. In other words: 'If you gain, you gain all; if you lose, you lose nothing.'

On balance, it is safer to invest a few hours in prayer and good works than flagrantly not to believe but later on discover that Christianity is true and you have missed out on your eternal reward. But is it this straightforward? Is belief a matter of choice? Perhaps for Pascal, because he was in doubt, the wager was enough to activate the believing part of himself and silence the unbelieving part. Starting from a position of non-belief, though, is it possible to choose to believe?

> 'If I saw no signs of a divinity, I would fix myself in denial. If I saw everywhere the marks of a Creator, I would repose peacefully in faith. But seeing too much to deny Him, and too little to assure me, I am in a pitiful state, and I would wish a hundred times that if a god sustains nature it would reveal Him without ambiguity.'
>
> Blaise Pascal, *Pensées*, 1669

Born into the faith

It used to be straightforward: if you lived in Europe, you were born into the Christian tradition, or perhaps into Judaism. There are places in the world where this type of religious observance still holds. But there are also people for whom the existence of God is no more in doubt than the existence of air. They no more choose to believe than you or I choose to breathe.

WHICH GOD ARE YOU CHOOSING?

Pascal's wager has a serious flaw, which Denis Diderot pointed out around 100 years later. Pascal has to choose not only whether to believe in God, but which god to believe in. If he picks the wrong god, the hours invested in prayer will have gone to waste and he'll still be damned forever.

Forced choices

William James, the brother of Henry James, the novelist, considered belief in God to be a 'forced choice' – one that we have to make, for or against, because there is no tenable intermediate position. He saw life as filled with choices, some of which are forced (have to be made) and some of which are momentous (they make an enormous difference to life). The choice, as he saw it, of whether or not to believe in God was both forced and momentous. He could see no reason why someone would choose unbelief, because religion gives a person a purpose in life, a moral framework and psychological structure – plus that ever-enticing bonus of an afterlife, of course.

Reason and faith, or reasons for faith?

There is an uneasy relationship between reason and faith. Some thinkers have argued that it is entirely reasonable to believe in God and have tried to defend His existence through reasoned argument.

But is there a philosophically robust rational argument for the existence of God? The theologian and philosopher St Anselm (1033–1109) is believed to be the originator of the ontological argument for the existence of God. This was based on the idea of God as a perfect being, which fact was itself a demonstration of God's existence: 'Nor do I seek to understand that I may believe, but I believe that I may understand. For this, too, I believe, that, unless I first believe, I shall not understand.' Later Voltaire claimed otherwise, saying that belief is a matter of reason: 'What is faith? Is it to believe that which is evident? No. It is perfectly evident to my mind that there exists a necessary, eternal, supreme, and intelligent being. This is no matter of faith, but of reason.'

But 'it is perfectly evident to my mind' is essentially a statement of faith. It may be 'evident' but it is only 'reasonable' if it can be proved by reason, by rational argument. And the only purpose of a logical proof of the existence of God is to persuade those who don't have faith, or whose faith is wavering – people like Pascal! To be fair to Voltaire, he believed that the universe was governed by immutable laws (what we would call the laws of physics) and these were innately explicable, even if we could not yet explain them. His belief in God was therefore more a matter of reason beyond current comprehension than an ineffable mystery.

Erasmus, a Dutch humanist writing in the early 16th century, was highly critical of the organized Church, which he believed obscured religion with unnecessary rituals and rules – he criticized the clergy for arguing all the way to Hell about how many knots to use when tying their sandals. Erasmus felt that simple, direct 'worship from the heart' was all that was required, and that it must be based in a confident recognition of God and the urge to worship Him. He considered belief in God to be a form of 'glorious folly' – folly precisely because it is accepted as true even if it seems counter to reason. It is beyond science, beyond reason – a simple affirmation of a directly perceived or apprehended truth. Søren Kierkegaard, too, saw belief as a 'leap of faith' and the very opposite of reason – if we could explain God, we would not need faith, so belief would be meaningless.

Can you taste tonic water?

This leaves those who don't believe with few options. Is it like the ability to taste tonic water? Some people can taste the bitterness of the quinine and some can't – it's a genetic difference. If you can't taste it, then you never will. Is faith the same? If you don't automatically have faith, are you excluded from the kingdom of heaven (assuming there is one)? According to many religious teachings, no amount of good works and charitable thought will help if the person does not have faith. John Calvin and his followers believed that God has already chosen those who will be saved. But according to more liberal doctrines we are all in with a chance.

The dominant modern attitude to religion, particularly in the West, is that it is a personal matter between the individual and God, perhaps with an intermediary spiritual leader. The German philosopher Friedrich Nietzsche (1844–1900) turned against religion – particularly Christianity – declaring it a sort of communal avoidance tactic for dealing with important social issues. In his view, religions that make a virtue of subservient positions such as poverty, humility and meekness endorse and prop up social systems that oppress the poor. He called them 'slave moralities' because they make a moral good of the characteristics that make people easy to exploit. The slaves are discouraged from rebelling against their condition because they are persuaded that the way they live is buying them favour in an afterlife that, in Nietzsche's view, is non-existent.

Psychoanalyst Sigmund Freud also saw an ulterior motive, but this time it was the subconscious seeking a source of comfort and nurturing. Humans, he felt, long for a 'father figure' to 'reconcile men to the cruelty of Fate . . . and compensate them for the sufferings [of] civilized life'. It is not people's reason or faith that drives them to God, according to Nietzsche and Freud, but a need to excuse their complacency in the face of abuse or suffering. They are not prompted by faith, or even by choice; instead they grasp at the straw of religion without much thought.

For some scientists, the incredible complexity of the universe leads towards rather than away from faith, as they feel it must reveal the hand of an intelligent creator.

CHAPTER 13

Does a dog have a soul?

Have you ever stared into the eyes of a dog and thought it must have a soul?

What is a soul?

People with religious beliefs often view the soul as the link between the human and a deity or creator. In the Abrahamic religions, the soul is the god-like part of the human, yearning to be like or to return to God, a reflection or fragment of the Holy Spirit. A non-religious view of the soul is that it's something akin to self-awareness or consciousness, or a part of a universal spirit (see Chapter 6).

Let God choose

For the religious, God has already decided whether animals have souls. But religious texts are notoriously cryptic, leaving a lot to interpretation and often giving contradictory messages. The Bible is not clear on the question of whether animals have souls. The following passage on the rapture, when Christ returns to Earth and carries away the saved, suggests that they do: 'The spirit of man that goeth upward, and the spirit of the beast that goeth downward to the earth.' (Ecclesiastes 3:21)

In Islam, animals are not considered to have free will – they will not be judged on their actions and admitted to heaven. So perhaps free will is a defining feature of being ensouled.

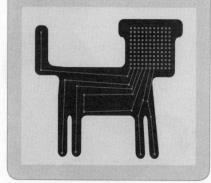

MIND-BODY DUALISM

René Descartes (1596–1650) saw the body as a mechanistic device inhabited by a soul. He believed only humans had souls, and that animals were empty, soulless machines.

One soul, pre-used

Buddhism does not endow even humans with a unique soul, but has all creatures partaking of a universal spirit. A similar view was held by Baruch Spinoza (1632–77), who saw a single spirit of nature inhabiting all creation – a view considered heretical and which saw him barred from the Jewish faith. Buddhism and Spinoza's view give each of us, and each dog, a little fragment of the universal soul, but not a fragment with any autonomy or meaningful independent existence.

For those who believe in the transmigration of souls – that a soul inhabits one body after another – a dog does have a soul. And a soul is not species-specific: the same soul can in one life inhabit a human and in another life a dog. Writing in the 5th century BC, Herodotus reported that the Ancient Egyptians thought the human soul was reborn as every type of animal, returning to human form again after 3,000 years. Some of the Ancient Greek philosophers, including Plato and Pythagoras, believed that a soul inhabits a body for only a short period of time. It rejoins a world of souls on the death of the body, until it inspires another body, either human or animal. In this scheme, a dog has exactly the same type and quality of soul as a human.

Are animals different?

The soul has often been seen as what produces consciousness, self-awareness, morality, a capacity for imagination, language, empathy, abstract thought, conscience, passion and hope. Many of these attributes or capabilities have traditionally been thought to distinguish humans from other animals. If what distinguishes humans from beasts is our ownership of a soul, then what defines a soul is that it belongs to a human and not a beast. It becomes a circular argument in which it is not possible for a dog to have a soul simply by virtue of being a dog: a soul is something that dogs don't have.

Increasing knowledge about animal physiology and behaviour casts doubt on age-old assumptions that there is something inherently special about the human being and the human brain (aside from any religious reason for considering humans special). We can detect intelligence and learning in other animals, some of which act in ways that in humans would be said to show compassion, fairness and altruism – and not only to members of their own group or species. Researcher Jean Decety found that rats would free other rats from traps even if they were not rewarded for doing so – and that they would free another rat in time for it to share a treat that the first rat could otherwise have eaten itself. Monkeys will also unlock a cage and free another monkey to share food. Stories of dolphins saving drowning sailors have circulated since Ancient Greek times, and several human infants have been raised by wild animals.

> 'Once when he was present at the beating of a puppy, he pitied it and said, "Stop, don't keep hitting him, since it is the soul of a man who is dear to me, which I recognized, when I heard it yelping."'
>
> Xenophanes, of Pythagoras (c.570–c.475BC)

Most people still assume that only humans create art, or feel remorse or guilt, fantasize, have hopes for the future or possess self-awareness and empathy. But there is no evidence either way – we don't *know* whether animals do these things. If they can do any or all of them, do they have souls?

The ensouled ark

In the Western world, dogs have a close relationship with humans. Cats and horses enjoy the same favour to a slightly lesser degree. We could argue that this has nothing to do with dogs (or cats or horses): it's about us, and our attitudes.

There are more intelligent animals than dogs, and other animals also show empathetic, altruistic and sharing behaviours. If a dog has a soul, so surely does a dolphin and a gorilla. Other animals are likely, biologically, to have similar levels of the mental behaviour we associate with souls.

> **ARISTOTLE'S CATALOGUE OF SOULS**
>
> Aristotle considered that fully featured souls are available only to humans. Animals can have a less rational soul. Plants can have only a bargain-basement soul.
> - 5* soul: suitable for humans only; capable of rational thought; locomotion and perception; life-sustaining functions.
> - 3* soul: suitable for animals; capable of locomotion and perception and life-sustaining functions.
> - 1* soul: suitable only for plants; no independent locomotion; basic life-sustaining functions only.

The English philosopher William Kingdon Clifford (1845–79) could not see how evolution made the jump from unconscious to conscious, so postulated that everything has some primitive form of consciousness which was then available for evolutionary development: 'It is impossible for anybody to point out the particular place in the line of descent where that event can be supposed to have taken place. The only thing that we can come to, if we accept the doctrine of evolution at all, is that even in the very lowest organism, even in the Amoeba which swims about in our own blood, there is something or other, inconceivably simple to us, which is of the same nature with our own consciousness.'

Does it matter?
Should it make a difference whether an animal has a soul or not? Just as Pythagoras asked that a puppy should not be kicked because he recognized a once-human soul in it, we might treat

animals differently if we knew they had souls. Most people feel we have more obligations to humans than to animals, more obligations to larger, possibly more intelligent animals than to – say – slugs and earwigs, and more obligations to animals than to plants. What – if any – special responsibilities do we have towards ensouled beings? Would our obligations towards animals and humans be the same if we knew animals had souls or were capable of something like our own levels of thought, empathy and suffering? And, as we don't know the answer to this question, should we give them the benefit of the doubt?

DOES A BEAN HAVE A SOUL?

It is reported that Pythagoras would not eat beans, and even allowed himself to be slaughtered rather than escape his pursuers by running through a field of beans and destroying them. One of the reasons suggested for this is that he believed beans played an important role in the transmigration of souls, perhaps acting as a conduit of some type between migrations.

CHAPTER 14

Can you say what you mean and mean what you say?

How reliable is language?

Over the last hundred years or so, philosophers have become very interested in language – in what we say, how words relate to their meanings and how we understand language when it is used by someone else. As all philosophical ideas must be communicated through language, the so-called 'linguistic turn' has had a big impact on what is said and how it is said, as well as giving rise to reflection on what can't be said. Does language limit what we can think, or even what exists?

> *"'Then you should say what you mean," the March Hare went on.*
> *"I do," Alice hastily replied; "at least – at least, I mean what I say – that's the same thing, you know."*
> *"Not the same thing a bit!" said the Hatter.*
>
> Lewis Carroll, *Alice's Adventures in Wonderland*, 1865

That thing is only a word

The problem of universals, whether or not concepts such as 'justice', 'childhood', 'anger' and 'red' exist, addresses the thorny issue of language. Some philosophers, called nominalists, believe there is no such 'thing' as anger, there is only behaviour that manifests anger, and the word, 'anger'. Other philosophers, called realists, claim that anger does exist as something separate from the word – people would continue to be angry even if we didn't have a word for it. Realists are further divided into those who, like Aristotle, believe that universals exist only as long as there is an example of them, and those who believe they exist anyway. So, for Aristotle, if people stopped being angry, or the human race was wiped out, then 'anger' would no longer exist. For Plato, an idealist, anger exists with or without people being angry as there is a 'form' (an ideal) for 'anger'.

What do words mean?

The question of how words accrue meaning interested the 20th-century German philosopher Ludwig Wittgenstein. For him, words are defined by how we use them. So if we start to use a word differently, its meaning changes. When young people began using 'cool' to mean something other than 'not very warm', the meaning of the word changed to match its new use. This represented a reversal for Wittgenstein, who said we must use language to make pictures or models of the world, which we can only do if the meaning of words is fixed in relation to things in the world. His later thinking centred around 'language games' in which people taking part in any discourse have to work out the meanings of the words as they are used.

So is there any correspondence between a word and its meaning, or is each word just an arbitrary sound to which we have assigned a meaning? Is there any good reason, for instance, why 'dog' should mean a canine mammal and not, say, an icicle or a carburettor? While there are logical relationships between words – ice and icicle, for example – only with a few onomatopoeic words is there any meaningful correspondence between word and thing or signifier and signified, as linguistic philosophers term them.

Ferdinand de Saussure saw the spoken word as the signifier, deeming the written word to be at another remove: the sound we associate with the letter 't' is the signified and the letter 't' is a signifier for it. The sound 't' is itself part of a sound pattern which we think of as a word, and the word is a signifier which we interpret as meaning the thing that is signified. The word 'tree' does not mean 'tree' in any absolute sense, but we agree to understand the concept 'tree' when we see or hear the word – as long as we know it is a word in English, of course.

Bring your baggage

Words come with lots of cultural baggage. This accumulates and changes over time and can even alter the meaning of written communications retrospectively. Mention the name

'Adolf' and most people will think of Hitler. If you wrote a story with a protagonist called Adolf, readers would bring certain expectations to it which you could either endorse or frustrate by the way you developed your character. The word 'gay' was used until the mid-20th century to mean cheerful and carefree, but now its primary meaning is 'homosexual'. No one can use the word in its original sense without the later sense colouring it. This also works retrospectively, so that the modern meaning of the word affects how we respond to a novel written in 1920.

The 20th-century British philosopher John Austin divided 'speech acts' (things that can be done with words) into three types: locutionary acts, illocutionary acts and perlocutionary acts. A locutionary act tells us something about the world. An illocutionary act can be a question, an instruction, a promise – it serves a special function beyond just telling us something. A perlocutionary act is language that is also a deed: saying 'I do' at a wedding, for instance. In order to understand how words function in these ways, everyone involved must know the cultural context in which they are used.

Do you know what I mean?

Some people see turquoise as a shade of blue and others see it as a shade of green. Are we sure we see it differently or do we just use the words differently? We can't really be sure that we all see red or yellow in the same way, but we agree to call the colour of blood 'red'. Similarly we might have different ideas of what we mean by anger, love, fear, or anything else. So what I mean when I say something is not necessarily what you understand when you hear it. Ironically, philosophers trying to talk about language find that the means of communication are too slippery, and not really up to the task.

The German philosopher Gottlob Frege (1848–1925) argued that language derives meaning only from context. If we take a sentence such as 'That pig is black', we can see it as something like a mathematical statement with an argument, 'that pig', and a function, 'is black'. We could take out the argument and replace it with another 'this cat', for instance. But the parts only have meaning when in a context – 'is black' doesn't tell us anything on its own.

A word alone has no meaning. Saussure explained that words are given meaning by virtue of the differences between them. So 'male' requires the existence of the word 'female', and to say something 'is' a cat is also to say that it's not a dog or a mouse or a wallaby. In a sense, everything is defined by what it is not.

Words and truth

It seems fairly obvious that we can use language to tell the truth or to lie. Bertrand Russell went further and said a statement can also be meaningless. A sentence such as 'The King of France is bald' is neither true nor false as there is no king of France. If we said it was false, that would imply that the king of France is not bald (but does exist). Then there can be totally perplexing statements, such as 'Everything I say is a lie', which if true is false, and if false is true.

Limiting thought

Language limits what we can say – but does it limit what we can think? There is an argument that it can. In Chinese, for example, when talking about a number of things, it's necessary to use a 'measure word' between the number and the object counted. So 'three maps' would effectively be 'three flat-things-that-are-maps'. The requirement to group things by one of their properties forges links between things and foregrounds one property over another. There is, in Chinese, more similarity between three maps and three stamps than between three maps and three gorillas. In English, the language doesn't reflect the fact that stamps are more like maps than like gorillas. We aren't forced to think about what things are like in order to count them.

Some languages have words for things that others don't. In Japanese, the word 'tsundoku' is the act of leaving a book unread after buying it. Although there isn't a word for that in English, the English also leave books unread. Do they think differently about the act, as there is no word for it? Is it easier to condone, because there is no word? Although not having a single word matters, it's still possible to say in English that you have bought a book and not read it. What about something we don't have a word for? We don't have a word for the way that a worm tunnels through the soil. We could describe the way it moves, involving muscular activity, but it's hard to imagine being a worm. Maybe one reason for this is that we don't have a word for what worms do. Or maybe we don't have a word for this activity because it's hard to imagine.

Languages – the same but different

Noam Chomsky suggests that all languages share some features of syntax (structure) and that our brains are hard-wired to learn languages using these patterns. It's as if the brain has a structure in place and just needs it to be populated with a language. Chomsky argues that any language is too complex for a child to pick up just by copying the people around him or her, and this indicates we have an innate language capability.

This children crossing sign shows stylized children – it's fairly easy to work out what it means even if you've never seen it before.

But the potential to learn seems to be time-limited. Some linguistics experts argue that there is a critical period during which language can be learned and if children are not exposed to a language during this period it will be difficult for them to learn one later on.

> *'Whereof one cannot speak, thereof one must be silent.'*
>
> Ludwig Wittgenstein, 1921

WILD THINGS

Throughout history there have been accounts of abandoned children brought up by wild animals, often wolves. On occasion, these feral children have been recovered and brought into human society. Studies show that they have difficulty acquiring human language if not exposed to it early on in life, but they can communicate with their animal carers. One of the more bizarre cases of a feral child is the Russian 'bird-boy'. He was kept by his mother in an aviary with birds, and she never spoke to him. When discovered at the age of seven, he communicated by chirping and flapping his arms.

Noam Chomsky

LANGUAGE WITHOUT WORDS

No one would suppose that small children or deaf and dumb people are incapable of thought, even though they cannot use language in the same way that adults who can speak and hear use language. 'Language' need not consist of spoken or written words. Some languages (Sanskrit, for instance) have only a written form, and others have only a spoken form. The Pirahã language can be 'spoken' entirely in whistles because it has only 13 distinct sounds and these can be replaced by whistle tones. And what about infograms? They communicate information without using words or established pictograms. Sign languages map visible movements to words, and the sign language that was developed for Helen Keller by her carer was based on movements which are felt. The possible forms of language extend far beyond speaking and writing.

The American author and political activist Helen Keller lost her sight and hearing as a result of illness in infancy. She triumphed against overwhelming odds and used her intelligence, courage, determination and influence to help others.

CHAPTER 15

How do you do the right thing?

The practical applications of philosophy are in deciding how to act.

Philosophy affects what we do in our daily lives, from which way we vote to whether we carry an organ donor card and how much we give to charity.

Making decisions

Søren Kierkegaard believed that the whole of life consisted of making choices; the dilemma for humans was how to choose between the range of possibilities on offer. 'What I really lack is to be clear in my mind what I am to do,' he said.

Some decisions are purely practical and have no philosophical dimension. Whether you will go to bed or stay up late to watch a movie might depend on whether you need to get up early to go to work the next day. But many decisions contain an ethical component – something that makes one choice morally better or worse than another. Philosophy can help you with any decision that involves the possibility of a morally right or wrong choice. So how do you go about making the right moral choices?

Follow the rules

We are surrounded by rules and regulations, including the laws of the land, religious rules, social rules and conventions, professional codes of practice, and rules set out by a landlord, parent, school, employer or other figure of authority or power. Some rules carry more weight than others. If we break the law, we can expect a judicial punishment, but if we violate social norms we might also attract disapproval. Don't underestimate the power of convention and tradition: a mother who failed to take her daughter to the foot-binder in 16th-century China would find she had an unmarriageable burden on her hands 20 years later (albeit one who was able to walk). We can be tyrannized by social 'rules' which have no legal force.

Religious rules are the only ones that claim specifically to be concerned with living a morally good life. They form 'value frameworks' which offer believers a short-cut to the right choice. If your religion tells you not to eat pork or not to lie, those are clear guidelines and you don't need to think hard about whether or not to do those things. How good or bad an act is can be determined by comparing it with the set of rules. Judging the morality of an action by reference to a set of rules or a sense of duty is called 'deontology', or 'deontological ethics'.

MORALS AND ETHICS

There is no substantial difference between the terms morals and ethics, though some philosophers distinguish between them. Both come from the same etymological root and they are often used interchangeably. 'Ethics' is more commonly used in theoretical contexts (such as 'ethics committee').

Does religion have a monopoly on morality?

Religion and morality have been closely linked for thousands of years. Some people argue that without religion there is no incentive to be moral. Why are religious people more likely to follow the moral law? Many religions offer a reward (such as salvation) to those who follow the rules, and might also threaten punishment (such as damnation) to try to frighten people into obedience. So perhaps believers follow the rules to get a reward or avoid a punishment, not because they want to be good.

> '*Either one's motives for following the moral word of God are moral motives, or they are not. If they are, then one is already equipped with moral motivations, and the introduction of God adds nothing extra. But if they are not moral motives, then they will be motives of such a kind that they cannot appropriately motivate morality at all . . . we reach the conclusion that any appeal to God in this connection either adds to nothing at all, or it adds the wrong sort of thing.*'
>
> Bernard Williams, 1972

Religions are good at bringing people together and getting them to follow a set of rules.

This doesn't sound a very moral position. Perhaps believers follow the rules because they love God and want to please him. In that case, the reward and punishment are unnecessary, so why are they such a significant feature of religious faith? By the same token, a non-believer could want to be good to please their fellow humans or because they love virtue. The humanist can be morally good without a reward or punishment, so perhaps the humanist is *more* moral than the religious believer. There is certainly no reason to suppose that morality is the preserve of the religious.

Religions are deontological. It is the duty of a believer to follow God's law. But there are lots of religions in the world, and they have different definitions of what it means to be 'good'. This means either that some (or all) religions are wrong or that what is 'right' for one person is not necessarily right for another. Of course, each believer will think his or her framework is the right one – so how is an outsider to choose between them?

Rules, schmules

If a moral framework has been properly constructed, it should guide us to do the right thing. But that's a big 'if'. Often, rules are designed to serve the best interests of those in power – even the moral codes at the heart of the major religions. Friedrich

Nietzsche thought Christianity served a political purpose and that it used the spurious promise of life after death to keep the oppressed obediently in their place. Some studies have found a direct correlation between crime and immoral behaviour and the presence of religion in a society, with higher crimes rates commensurate with a higher level of religious belief or practice. This suggests that rules alone don't make people behave in a moral way.

We all occasionally encounter conflicting duties or obligations or face problems that force us to make difficult choices. Sometimes the rules we follow will require a course of action we feel unable to make. We might have to evaluate conflicting claims and choose the one we consider the most important or

> 'You find this curious fact, that the more intense has been the religion of any period and the more profound has been the dogmatic belief, the greater has been the cruelty and the worse has been the state of affairs. . . . You find as you look around the world that every single bit of progress in humane feeling, every improvement in the criminal law, every step toward the diminution of war, every step toward better treatment of the coloured races, or every mitigation of slavery, every moral progress that there has been in the world, has been consistently opposed by the organized churches of the world.'
>
> Bertrand Russell, 1957

The pansy is the symbol of free thought, the philosophical position that says people should base their thinking and decisions on reason and logic, free from bias, tradition, custom, authority and any other type of intellectual pressure.

How do you do the right thing? **117**

most compelling. If you follow a religion, you might not be able to see how to apply its code to a complex problem, or you might disagree with it if it doesn't seem to apply to your circumstances (see Chapter 16). You might seek help from a spiritual adviser, or you might be thrown back on your own resources.

ASK YOURSELF

Philosophers like to use thought experiments to test theories. Try these three thought experiments to see how your own values help you to make tricky decisions.

- You are driving a car with three passengers. There has been a landslide and the road ahead is blocked. There is not time to stop before you hit the rocks in your path, but you could swerve down a side road. Unfortunately, there is a young man in the middle of the narrow road. If you take the turning you will certainly strike him. Do you turn into the narrow road, killing the man who would otherwise have lived? Or do you stay on your original course, possibly killing all four people in the car?

- You need a new shirt to go to a job interview, but you don't have much money. The only place you can afford to buy a shirt is in a store that sells cheap goods. You have seen a documentary about the store and know that the shirts are made by exploited workers overseas. You don't want to endorse the poor treatment of the workers, but you need a shirt. What do you do?

- You find evidence that your country's government is horribly corrupt. You will be in danger if you reveal what you have discovered, but many people will suffer as a consequence of the corruption if you don't. Do you reveal it?

Are there right and wrong answers to these questions? Are they the same for everyone in all circumstances?

You can only make difficult moral decisions if you know your own values, how you arrived at them, how you can defend them and how they fit together. There will also be times when terrible things happen. You will need a way of accommodating them into your world view and value framework, or you will need to adjust your views to take account of them.

Ways of deciding – using some 'isms'

The English philosopher Henry Sidgwick (1838–1900) found that the ways in which people made ethical decisions, if they were not following rules, fell into three categories: egoism, utilitarianism, and intuitionism.

Egoism is choosing the option that will bring you the most pleasure and least pain, regardless of the impact it has on other people. This doesn't sound like a path to a moral life. It might be attractive to start with, but it will probably go wrong as people won't want to be around you if you are selfish.

Utilitarianism judges how moral an action is by weighing up the total pleasure and pain it brings to all the people concerned (see Chapter 21). An act is moral if it produces more pleasure than pain to the many, and immoral if it produces more pain than pleasure. It is quite a good starting point, but it's not infallible. It is also sometimes difficult to do the calculation and even more difficult to follow the path that the calculation shows to be the best.

Intuitionism depends on us intuitively knowing what is right and wrong – a gut feeling, or common sense. Sidgwick felt intuitionism and utilitarianism went well together, because our instinctive choices often seem to depend on a feeling that something that harms people is wrong.

Ethical decisions – should, shouldn't and may

An ethical decision is one that requires you to decide what is the right or moral thing to do, or decide to do what is right or avoid what is wrong. For example, if you find an envelope of money left on a table in a library, you probably know that you should hand it in. But then you have to decide whether you actually will hand it in. You might persuade yourself that it will never be returned to the rightful owner so you might as well keep it yourself as let someone else keep it. You might feel that people who leave money lying around only have themselves to blame if it's not returned to them. Or you might hand it in, regardless of what will happen to it, because you consider it wrong to keep it.

What would you do if you found an anonymous envelope full of banknotes? Would you hand it in or keep it?

Acts can be divided into three categories for the purpose of moral judgement:

- **Things that are required** – in other words, you must do them
- **Things that are permitted** (but not required) – in other words, you may do them (or not)
- **Things that are forbidden** – in other words, you must not do them.

Some acts meet pretty universal agreement. Most people would say that murder is bad, so it falls into the category of forbidden acts – you *must not* murder people. But in a lot of cases there is disagreement about the moral status of an act. For some people, eating some types of food is forbidden, whereas for others it is permitted and is an act that has no particular moral status, good or bad.

Occasionally, there can be complete disagreement between people. Some people consider the circumcision of infants and young children to be ethically required because their faith demands it; others say it is permissible; and some say it is a violation of the body of someone who has not given their permission, so it is morally wrong and should be forbidden. Arguments about ethical issues can become heated and even violent. When they are connected to religious beliefs, they can lead to wars that last for centuries.

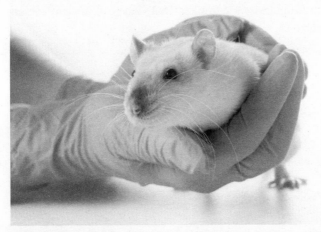

Sometimes the logic of morality can be complicated. Is it right or wrong to use animals to test medicines? Animal rights protesters would say it was definitely wrong. But is it acceptable to risk harm to humans by not testing medicines on animals?

What does happen and what should happen

We all live in societies that have cultural norms, often reflected in the law. A lot of the time, we are fairly confident that what we should do is obey the law, but sometimes this may conflict with what we feel is right. Just because something *does* happen doesn't mean it *should* happen.

Two hundred years ago, many people in the USA kept slaves. This doesn't mean slavery is or was right – but the situation only changed because enough people decided that slavery was wrong. In order for societies to make progress, someone has to want to overturn the apple cart; someone has to decide that what *does* happen is not what *should* happen. Then they go about trying to change it.

If you are in the position of thinking that things should be changed, you will need a good basis for your own moral thinking so that you can explain it to others and persuade them. Before you can really decide what to do, you need to know what you think and why you think it. That's where philosophy comes in handy.

CHAPTER 16

Should we ever burn witches?

Is what is right or wrong always so?
Or does it differ depending on the
times and circumstances?

Why is good 'good'?

Is what is right and just always the same? And why is what is good 'good' anyway?

We spend a lot of effort deciding which actions are good, but most of us give little thought to what we mean by 'good' or 'moral'. The 20th-century British philosopher George Moore concluded that 'good' isn't something we can define. We all have some innate sense of what is right and what is wrong. Moore said that we don't need to approach the nature of 'good' through science or ethics: we just know that it is 'a simple notion, just as "yellow" is a simple notion . . . you cannot explain what good is.' This might sound like a bit of a cop-out because it doesn't give us a clue as to where this feeling comes from or whether it is likely to be the same for all people.

BIG QUESTIONS: META-ETHICS

There are three distinct categories of ethics which philosophers consider:

- **Meta-ethics** concerns the over-arching questions of the nature of good and how we can distinguish between good and evil, whether what is good is good at all times and in all places, and whether 'good' even exists.
- **Normative ethics** concerns what people should think is good or bad – so whether jealousy is bad, giving to charity is good, and so on.
- **Applied ethics** concerns the application of ethics to life, governing how we should live and what we should do. It takes the principles established by normative ethics and puts them into practice. There are several branches of applied ethics. For instance, bioethics deals with issues such as whether we should use human embryos in medical research and whether we should produce genetically modified organisms.

One suggestion is that the definition of good is that which would seem good to an ideal observer – a hypothetical being with complete knowledge and an absolute command of reason. Another proposal is that it is whatever an omniscient being (some kind of a God) would consider good. This gives rise to the 'divine command' theory – the notion that things are good or bad according to what a God has commanded. It doesn't quite answer the question, though, as it leads us to ask: has the God commanded it because it is good or is it good only because the God has commanded it? If the first, there is still a source of 'good' that lies outside this God since he doesn't have any choice over what to say is good. If the second, it all looks rather arbitrary, as anything the God had commanded would be good – including burning witches – but it's something we wouldn't condone today.

Relying on divine command introduces another problem. Different people follow different religions – it can't be the case that all the divine beings are the ultimate arbiters of morality. Most people would say that only one religion (their own, of course) has set the correct moral framework. The fact that there are different beliefs doesn't mean the divine command theory is wrong, but it does make it harder to deal with. If we can't say why good is good, it's worth wondering whether it's anything at all – does 'good' even exist? This is part of the larger issue of whether universals – abstract concepts – exist.

Are there moral facts?

It's difficult to say whether ethics is based in anything 'true'. Most people assume there are ways in which things in the physical world work – that there is a particular arrangement of planets in the solar system, for instance, or that the body processes sugars and fats in certain ways. There are 'out-there' truths about these matters. Is the same true of ethics? Are there any 'out-there' truths that can be discovered about how to live a moral life? Some philosophers say there are ideals of justice, truth, morality and so on which are independent of people and societies (and gods) – perhaps something like the innate idea which Moore mentioned, or perhaps dwelling in some realm

AH, BUT WHAT IS 'TRUE'?

Philosophy, naturally, also addresses the question of what we mean by 'true'. There are two significant, competing theories.

The correspondence theory of truth is that in order to be true a statement must correspond to something verifiable in the real world. This is what most people mean by 'true'. So a statement such as 'deciduous trees lose their leaves in autumn' is true. A statement such as 'deciduous trees are beautiful in autumn' is not true because some people find trees beautiful and others do not.

The coherence theory of truth is harder to explain and understand. This says that there must be a coherent system in which statements are true in relation to one another, and individual statements can only be true if they have a place in the system. In this model, quantum physics and classical physics (which have elements that contradict one another) can both be 'true' as systems. Statements in quantum theory are only true in the context of that theory. So we could say 'particles widely separated from one another can act together instantaneously' and in the context of quantum physics that is true because the system logically supports it, whether or not the system itself is a correct model of the universe.

A statement like 'Thou shalt not kill' is not true in the correspondence model. It tries to make the world conform to its idea by presenting a statement of fact: you will not kill people. If someone does then kill another person, the statement becomes untrue. In the coherence version of truth, the statement 'Thou shalt not kill' could be true.

of ideas like Plato's world outside the cave. In this case, there is something which is 'good', and we have to discover what it is.

An alternative possibility is that there is no such thing as 'good' or 'bad' and any statement of the type 'killing is wrong' or 'killing is good' is untrue. These statements can still have meaning even without being 'true'. We might take 'killing is wrong' to be prescriptive, meaning 'we must not kill people', or we might take it as emotional, expressing disapproval – 'we don't like killing'. It might be better to rephrase 'killing is wrong' to show exactly what we mean: 'don't kill people', or 'we disapprove of killing people'.

One size fits all?

Is there any kind of genuine, universal moral code that lies behind this rule-making? Are some things always right or wrong? Would it be possible to extract a set of rules that could and should be applied in all times and places?

If there is some overall 'out-there' moral framework which we have to discover, then morality is absolute – it doesn't change with time and place. If there is not a single moral code, morality is relative – it varies between cultures.

This has implications for how we view and treat other people and other cultures, and is increasingly important as our societies become more multi-cultural. How far should we respect, endorse and protect the moral views of others?

All change?

In Ancient Greece it was normal for people to keep slaves and for adult men to have sex with young boys. These things were not considered wrong. Does that mean they were wrong but no one recognized it? Or that this type of behaviour was not wrong for that society, but is for ours? If we take an absolutist stance, either the Ancient Greeks were wrong to be slave-owning pederasts or we are being unnecessarily generous to our fellow human beings in not following their example. If we take a relativist stance, it was all right for the Ancient Greeks to do those things, but it's not now OK for us to do them.

It's difficult to step outside our own social context to see how the moral situation might be seen by others. Perhaps in two

BURNING THOSE WITCHES

For a believer, there is a specific intention behind God's words which should be good for all time. Religions endeavour to reveal and promote that intention. But religious texts are notoriously ambiguous, cryptic or contradictory, and countless religious wars have sprung from the different interpretations of what the rules mean. So 'Thou shalt not suffer a witch to live' was taken literally in the 17th century, but is illegal now (it was often illegal then, by the way). It has been estimated that between 1500 and 1800, around 200,000 convicted 'witches' were executed in the Western world.

If the people who burned witches genuinely believed them to be guilty, was the act immoral? Do moral relativism and intentionalism constitute a defence for witch-burning?

hundred years' time, our descendants will wonder that anyone ever considered it acceptable to eat animals or to exploit the environment to the extent we do, or to have alcohol and tobacco as legal drugs. Or there might be some other objection that we can't even imagine right now.

The humanist view

The first Western philosopher to propose a form of cultural relativism was the 16th-century French essayist Michel de Montaigne. Writing at a time when explorers were bringing back tales of the strange ways in which people lived in newly discovered lands, Montaigne argued for tolerance: 'The laws of conscience, which we say are born of nature, are born of custom. Each man, holding in inward veneration the opinions and behaviour approved and accepted around him.'

Montaigne didn't believe that all moral codes and judgements were equally valid, but that every individual should examine and reflect on the behaviour appropriate in any particular context. This humanist view gives each person the authority to decide what he or she considers moral, as long as they reflect upon the question intelligently.

Lines in the sand

As soon as we allow different moral codes, the qualities of tolerance and consideration become significant issues. Being tolerant of and considerate towards different views is often easy – it would be churlish and inconsiderate for a non-Muslim to disregard a Muslim colleague's observance of Ramadan, for instance. Trickier questions arise when one person's moral rules harm or infringe the rights of other people.

> 'The day may come when the rest of the animal creation may acquire those rights which never could have been witholden from them but by the hand of tyranny. The French have already discovered that the blackness of the skin is no reason a human being should be abandoned without redress to the caprice of a tormentor. It may one day come to be recognized that the number of the legs, the villosity [hairiness] of the skin, or the termination of the os sacrum [tail] are reasons equally insufficient for abandoning a sensitive being to the same fate.'
>
> Jeremy Bentham, 1789

Some of the people who would criticize terrible working conditions in their own countries may buy cheap clothes made in foreign sweatshops. Is this morally consistent? Are poor working conditions abroad acceptable because the alternative – poverty and starvation – is worse? Or is this just an argument we make to salve our consciences?

Female genital mutilation (FGM) is generally considered abhorrent and immoral outside the group that practises it. The view that it is acceptable in some societies might itself be considered immoral. Many leading figures in Islam have spoken against it, but the groups that practise FGM – which they prefer to call female genital surgery – defend their right to continue with it.

At what point is someone's right to different beliefs no longer supported? Is there a difference between banning FGM in Europe and trying to stop it in countries such as Somalia and Ethiopia, where it is common? Do we have a right to try to impose our morality on other cultures? Or do we, perhaps, have a moral *obligation* to try to impose our view on other cultures in some cases? (The World Health Organization passed a resolution banning FGM in 1994.)

IS RELIGION A SPECIAL CASE?

The *shechita* method of slaughter required for Jewish food is incompatible with the practice of stunning animals to make slaughter more humane. In some countries, exceptions are made to the legal requirement to stun animals when slaughtering them by Jewish or Islamic traditional methods. This compromise prioritizes religious sensibilities over animal rights. But is this the right thing to do? In what way is religion 'special', if it is at all?

In the Middle Ages, European Crusaders slaughtered thousands of innocent non-Christians in the name of bringing them to the 'true' faith and saving them from damnation (though, more accurately, the Crusades were an excuse for large-scale pillage and looting). A Crusader who genuinely believed in the propaganda would have felt a moral obligation to go on a Crusade and 'save souls'.

The wearing of symbols or clothes with religious significance was banned in schools in France in 2004. Widely interpreted as a law banning the Muslim headscarf (khimar), it also applies to crucifixes and turbans.

The opposite of rules

While fixed moral codes help to make life simpler, they can also lead to dilemmas when the rules don't seem right, or don't take account of the context. The approach taken in many situations in which moral decisions have to be made officially is one called 'casuistry'. In this, each case is treated independently and reviewed in the light of all knowledge, circumstances, likely outcomes and context to reach a decision that seems right. Casuistry operates within a legal framework, but does not have to follow any set of strict moral rules. It is the approach used by medical ethics committees, for example, when deciding on courses of treatment for individual patients. Because the circumstances of each patient differ, cases that look very similar may have different outcomes.

Our instinctive responses to moral issues often make reference to context. Casuistry formalizes this. Suppose a couple with no children want state-funded IVF to enable them to have a child, and a couple who already have three children also want IVF. The childless couple is likely to be prioritized. But now suppose the childless couple are indigent alcoholics and the three children of the other couple all have a fatal hereditary condition. Now we might prioritize the couple with the three existing children.

Just one rule

One way of approaching the question of what is right and wrong is to consider what you would want to happen to yourself if you were on the receiving end of someone else's moral choice. It's not infallible, as people have different priorities and preferences, but it's a good start.

Often called the Golden Rule, it has been proposed by many philosophers and religions since the time of Ancient Babylon. It is a doctrine of reciprocity, meaning that it is a two-way relationship that sets out both your obligations to others and theirs to you. There are positive and negative statements of it:

- Treat others as you would like others to treat you.
- Don't treat others in ways that you would not like to be treated.

Immanuel Kant intended something similar when he said in 1785: 'Act only according to that maxim whereby you can, at the same time, will that it should become a universal law.' Kant called his rule

'The reality of the world today is that grounding ethics in religion is no longer adequate. This is why I am increasingly convinced that the time has come to find a way of thinking about spirituality and ethics beyond religion altogether.'

Tenzin Gyatso, the fourteenth Dalai Lama, 2012

the 'categorical imperative'. He denied that it was the same as the Golden Rule, though, as it has no element of reciprocity – it's not to do with what *you* want and how *you* would like to be treated, but about what would be best for everyone.

'A man should be hanged only for stealing the shoes of children sent barefoot to their death in gas chambers.'

Martha Gellhorn on the trial of Adolf Eichmann, 1962

Does 'I didn't mean to' make a difference?

Should you be judged for your intentions as well as the consequences of your actions?

We have all at some time done something that has unintentionally hurt or upset someone else. Perhaps you have pleaded, 'but I didn't mean to', hoping to defuse the situation. And we have all been unintentionally hurt by someone else's actions. How did we feel when they said, 'but I didn't mean to'? Just how much do intentions count?

Intentions and consequences

Consider this scenario: two reckless friends go out drinking and then drive home separately. One knocks down a woman and kills her. The other drives through a red light on an empty road and is stopped by the police. The first is imprisoned for causing death by reckless driving. The second is fined and banned from driving. On the same day, a man has an argument with his wife. When she leaves the house, he gets into his car and follows her, then deliberately runs her over. He gets a long jail sentence for murder.

The first two drivers had the same intention – to get home quickly without spending money on a cab – but the consequences of their identical acts were very different. The third driver had a different intention – to harm his wife – but the consequences were the same as those of one of the drivers in the first case. How should we rate intentions and consequences when we assess the morality of these acts? Should one drunk driver get a longer sentence because he was unlucky and encountered a pedestrian? Or should another drunk driver get a lighter sentence because he was lucky enough not to? Should the driver with murderous intent get a longer sentence than the drunk driver, although the consequences were the same?

Do intentions count?

According to Immanuel Kant, the outcome of an act does not really matter as long as our intentions are good. So if a person throws himself into a river to save a drowning person, he is worthy of praise whether or not he saves the person. Even badly thwarted intentions still count. If someone tries to do good but inadvertently does harm, the act is a good one because the intentions were good. Similarly, if someone intends to do a bad deed but it misfires and has a beneficial outcome, the deed remains immoral.

It's all about you

Kant's is an intentionalist view – the morality of an act begins and ends with the intentions behind it. This makes every act about the perpetrator and not about the person or people affected. Judging the act is then judging the person who carries it out. Exactly the same act can be deemed more or less morally good depending on the intentions behind it. If we took a purely intentionalist view, both drunk drivers would be treated in the same way – either both banned, or both jailed.

Suffer the consequences

The opposite view is consequentialist – the outcome (consequence) is supremely important in deciding how we judge the act. In a purely consequentialist scheme, the intention behind an act is irrelevant. In some ways this appeals to our sense of fairness. It means the drunk driver who kills someone is punished more harshly than the drunk driver who doesn't because he or she has caused more harm.

The act of drunk-driving fits into a larger scheme of justice, retribution and deterrence. We need our legal penalties to take account of both the actual and the *possible* consequences. Too light a penalty suggests an offence isn't serious. It leaves victims feeling undervalued and doesn't deter others from the same act. But penalties that are too severe backfire. If everyone convicted of drunk-driving were sentenced as though they had killed someone, it would lead to other crimes – such as people fleeing the scene of even a minor accident.

SIR GOWTHER: HERO OR VILLAIN?

The medieval story of Sir Gowther tackles the intentionalist/consequentialist dilemma head on. Sir Gowther is conceived when his mother is raped by a devil. As an infant, he carries out all kinds of heinous deeds, such as pushing nuns off cliffs. This is easy to account for – he is, after all, spawn of the devil. His behaviour doesn't improve as he grows older. Eventually, someone explains to Gowther that he is bad because he is demonic, so he is just acting out his fate. This greatly troubles him as his sole ambition is to act in a shocking, perverse way. In order to be as contrary as possible, he resolves to behave well. Thereafter, he does good deeds and defies everyone's expectations.

Are Gowther's deeds morally good? His intention was not to do good, but to act perversely by doing good.

The belief that the death penalty was unfair led to a refusal to impose it. Juries began to find clearly guilty people not guilty, and sentences passed were often commuted or abandoned: of 35,000 death sentences handed down in 1770–1830, only

THE BLOODY CODE

During the 18th century, the death penalty was imposed for an ever-increasing number of crimes in Britain. By 1800, there were 220 capital crimes, including 'being in the company of Gypsies for one month', 'strong evidence of malice in a child aged 7–14 years of age' and 'using a disguise whilst committing a crime'. The penalty was intended to have a deterrent effect; as George Savile said in the 17th century, 'Men are not hanged for stealing horses, but that horses may not be stolen.'

7,000 were carried out. Instead of passing the death penalty, courts began to impose transportation – compulsory relocation to Australia, which was then a British colony. The law was reformed in 1823, removing the death penalty for all crimes except murder and treason.

How do we judge the consequences?

How do we judge whether consequences are good or bad, and who makes that judgement? It can involve weighing up the effects on different people or groups – a utilitarian approach. There might also be long-term and short-term consequences that cast an action in different lights.

LESSONS FROM ANCIENT CHINA

In the 5th century BC, the Chinese philosopher Mozi proposed the earliest form of consequentialism. He did not pay attention to the good of individuals, but looked at the consequences of an action in terms of its effect on the whole of society. Society benefited from stable social order, sufficient wealth and population increase. As he lived in a time of frequent wars and famines, population growth was an important consideration if a state was to survive rather than be overrun by neighbouring states.

Consequences can be more or less predictable. Sometimes, it's impossible for someone to foresee the consequences of their actions. Suppose that as a small child, Adolf Hitler had fallen into a river and a passing good Samaritan saved the boy. In the short term, this is a good action with good consequences, and the child's saviour could expect praise. But with the benefit of hindsight we might say it would have been better to let little Adolf drown if the consequences of saving him included the World War II and the Holocaust. Surely no one can be blamed for not being able to predict the distant future? A hard-line consequentialist would say that an act is wrong if the consequences are bad, no matter whether they were foreseen by anyone. But few people would leave a child to drown on the off-chance that he might grow up to be a war criminal.

Now suppose that you buy a cheap toy for a child. It is badly made and faulty, but you don't notice. It breaks and the child is hurt. The consequences were foreseeable – someone else might have noticed that the toy was faulty – but they weren't foreseen or intended. Was the act morally bad? What if you did notice the toy was faulty but didn't think it would matter? Then the consequences were foreseeable and foreseen but not intended. Was it wrong to give the child the toy? Only if you had expected the child to be hurt by the toy would the consequences be foreseeable, foreseen *and* intended.

Who should be working out the likely consequences? If we leave it to each individual, the wiser person will be regarded as more culpable for their mistakes as they would be deemed better able to foresee consequences. Some philosophers suggest that a hypothetical knowledgeable but impartial observer should be the judge. This is rather like the ideal juror in English law as 'the man on the Clapham omnibus' – a fairly normal person with no axe to grind, no psychosis that might lead to an odd judgement, and so on. Other philosophers say that only an omniscient observer can really judge. This makes it difficult for anyone to be sure they have taken sufficient care in assessing the likely consequences of their actions.

The first position is more liberal, and therefore workable, allowing that if someone has taken due care to discover the likely consequences, they are acting responsibly. The chance of causing an accident by driving after drinking is not particularly remote. The drunk driver is therefore negligent in ignoring the risk as a knowledgeable observer would have been able to foresee the accident. The chance of a child you save from drowning growing up to become a war criminal is slight and unforeseeable, so fishing Adolf from the river is still a good act.

The conclusion of consequentialism is that no act is innately right or wrong, as its outcome will determine its morality. Even acts that look incontestably immoral could be right in some circumstances.

Should we just follow the rules?

Life would be tedious if we had to consider the likely and possible consequences of every act. Instead we can use the shortcut of referring to the legal or religious rules society has put in place. This is called 'rule consequentialism'. Our rule systems are generally based on a consequentialist approach: we devise rules on the basis of what might happen in various circumstances. These expectations are derived from past experience. As drunk driving frequently has a bad outcome, it is illegal. But there are circumstances in which the rules are not a very good guide. Every country has a law against killing people – but if a gunman were to open fire on a classroom full of school children and the teacher were to kill him to protect them, the teacher would be considered a hero.

Assessing acts individually is called 'act consequentialism'. The teacher who kills the gunman is following this approach. As a day-to-day basis for choosing how to act, it's not very practical as each person must assess the likely and possible outcomes of each act before doing anything. Life would be very slow and unpredictable as people would assess situations and acts and come to different conclusions.

> '*The best argument for rule-consequentialism is that it does a better job than its rivals of matching and tying together our moral convictions, as well as offering us help with our moral disagreements and uncertainties.*'
>
> Brad Hooker, Professor of Philosophy, University of Reading

In some cases, the delay in deciding would itself produce a bad outcome. A person with practical wisdom would make better choices than an inexperienced, younger or less wise person, so the effectiveness would be uneven. Many people would prioritize beneficial consequences to themselves and their families, while rule consequentialism prioritizes benefits to the community as a whole or to the majority. In exceptional cases, such as the teacher facing the gunman, act consequentialism can give the best result.

A compromise position is two-level consequentialism, associated with the philosophers R.M. Hare and Peter Singer. This combines act consequentialism and rule consequentialism. If the consequences of an act can be reliably foreseen, act consequentialism holds. If the consequences are too difficult to predict, rule consequentialism steps in.

THE ACTS AND OMISSIONS DOCTRINE

In some cases, acts and failures-to-act are seen as equivalent in moral terms. So if you could save someone by not doing something – such as revealing their whereabouts to criminals who are looking for them – then omitting to act is a moral act of the same type as giving them a hiding place. But in some cases, acts and omissions are treated differently. In medical ethics, for example, the same outcome – the death of a terminally ill patient – could result from withholding treatment, or turning off life-support, or putting a pillow over the patient's face. A medical ethics committee might approve either of the first two, but not the third. The first is an omission, the third is an act, and the second is somewhere in between – an omission that becomes an act.

CHAPTER 18

Is all fair in love and war?

When we excuse doing wrong by saying that the ends justify the means, is this true? Or is it a recipe for violent tyranny?

Ends and means

The view that the morality of an action depends on its consequences is called, unsurprisingly, consequentialism (see Chapter 17). When we talk about the ends justifying the means, the ends are the intended consequences.

Whether the ends justify the means will depend on:

- whether the ends were justifiable anyway
- whether the ends were achieved
- the means that were employed.

Suppose one state invades another with the intention of deposing a terrible dictator (set aside, for the moment, the question of whether that state has any right to involve itself in the internal affairs of the other). If the invading state achieves its aim quickly and with no bloodshed, few will regret the action. But if the invading state kills 100,000 civilians in its quest for liberation, do the ends justify the means? What if the invading state kills 100,000 civilians and still fails to overthrow the despot? Although the intention was the same, the consequences are different.

Is there such a thing as a just war?

When is war justified? It might be nice to say that it's never justified, but most people would accept that if no one was prepared even to defend themselves we'd soon be overrun by tyrants. The idea of justifying war is an old one. It aims to reconcile two conflicting principles:

- that it's wrong to kill people
- that states have a duty to defend their citizens and justice.

Sometimes, force and violence seem to be the only way to defend innocent lives.

The Roman orator Cicero argued that the only acceptable reason for war was just vengeance or self-defence, in which he included the defence of honour.

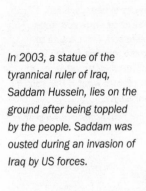
In 2003, a statue of the tyrannical ruler of Iraq, Saddam Hussein, lies on the ground after being toppled by the people. Saddam was ousted during an invasion of Iraq by US forces.

Cicero said that a war could only be justified if it had been declared and if compensation for wrongs had been sought and refused. War should be the action of last resort.

St Augustine felt that war was always sinful, but also recognized that wars will always happen. He decided that they were sometimes allowable as long as they were waged to stop sin. This could mean driving back invaders, deposing cruel despots, and so on. But the term 'sin' is problematic. The Crusaders believed that Muslims were sinful infidels and if a war of religion could convert them it would be stopping sin. This justification clearly wouldn't be acceptable now. Every religion could make the same point – we would be forever fighting in order to prevent the 'sin' of people following the wrong religion. St Augustine also allowed war as a punishment, which would not now be considered just cause. Neither Cicero nor St Augustine would sanction a war waged for reasons of cruelty or a desire to extend a state's territory.

St Augustine considered a war justified if it was the lesser of two evils – if it prevented or halted a greater evil. St Thomas Aquinas, 800 years later, examined the means employed in war – the '*jus in bello*'. During the 16th century, the principles that have become pretty much universal were established.

> '*We do not seek peace in order to be at war, but we go to war that we may have peace. Be peaceful, therefore, in warring, so that you may vanquish those whom you war against, and bring them to the prosperity of peace.*
>
> '*A just war is wont to be described as one that avenges wrongs, when a nation or state has to be punished, for refusing to make amends for the wrongs inflicted by its subjects, or to restore what it has seized unjustly.*'
>
> St Augustine, 4th century

THE ELEMENTS OF A JUST WAR

A war can only be considered just if it fulfils two requirements:

- *Jus ad bellum:* the use of military force is justified
- *Jus in bello:* conduct in war is ethical – for example, prisoners are treated fairly.

Judging the ends

To judge whether the ends are good, we need to be able to measure 'good'. This isn't as straightforward as it sounds. On the whole, it's better to be alive than dead, better to be free than in prison (unless free people are starving and prisoners are fed). But some other things are debatable. Should we overthrow a dictator to bring democracy to a country? Who is to say that democracy is a good thing?

Extraordinary measures

In times of war and emergency, different rules often operate. Soldiers are shot for deserting, looters are shot for ransacking earthquake rubble or shops left unprotected, and innocent people are interrogated or imprisoned in case they might pose a national threat. During World War II, Japanese residents in the USA and Italian residents in the UK were moved to internment camps even though there was no evidence to suggest that they were working for the enemy. Most people felt this was the lesser of two evils – that there was less harm in imprisoning innocent people than perhaps jeopardizing a whole population. It is a utilitarian way of deciding whether the ends justify the means.

An alternative measure is not even to try to justify the means. Some political philosophers have argued that, in war, any means are justified if the end (the reason for the war) is justified. If innocent civilians have to die to secure a speedy victory, so be it. Others believe some acts, such as the bombing of hospitals, can never be justified. In practical terms, the brutality of war often overtakes ethical positions. Some philosophers have taken a pragmatic view and said that ethical judgements can't be applied in war. Others have gone further and said that war lies outside the scope of ethics altogether.

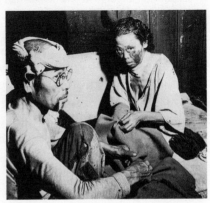

Casualties of the atomic bombing of Japan at the end of World War II. Can the massive human cost of nuclear weapons be justified in any military cause?

The dictator's viewpoint

Niccolò Machiavelli, writing for the guidance of political leaders in *The Prince*, believed the ends always justified the means as long as the ends were the right ends.

For a prince (political leader) this meant keeping power. Machiavelli was amoral rather than immoral. The measures he recommended were directed solely at being a successful ruler. He ruled out despotism, not because it is wrong but because despots attract enemies and are likely to be overthrown.

> *'A new prince cannot escape a name for cruelty, for he who quells disorder by a few signal examples will, in the end, be the more merciful.'*
>
> Niccolò Machiavelli, 1532

IS TORTURE EVER JUSTIFIED?

The use of measures such as 'waterboarding' and 'extraordinary rendition' – whereby suspects are sent to countries where torture is allowed – call into question the type of behaviour allowed in a war and the means that might or might not be justified in securing ends.

It's possible to make a utilitarian argument in favour of the use of torture. If it can elicit information that will protect innocent people, the harm to the tortured prisoner might be offset by the greater benefit. Arguments against torture can be pragmatic (it doesn't work) or ethical. One argument is that our own moral standing is reduced by engaging in unethical behaviours such as torture – that is, it's spiritually damaging to the perpetrator. Those in favour of using torture often call it something else, such as 'enhanced interrogation techniques'. This acknowledges that torture is considered unacceptable (and illegal under international treaties), and attempts to deflect bad publicity. Does dishonesty just compound the immorality?

CHAPTER 19

Could we make a perfect society?

Will the poor always be with us?
Or could we create a world that is
fair to all?

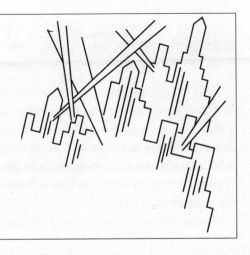

Most of us grumble about modern society and our own particular national and regional governments – that's nothing new. Every administration in history might have had 'could do better' written on its report card. But could any society ever do well enough?

Imagining the city

It's 2,400 years since Plato wrote *The Republic*, in which he examined how best to govern a hypothetical state. Plato's model had philosopher kings in charge, with considerable constraints on what they could do. In his view, only philosophers can see the 'form' (metaphysical ideal) of justice, and this makes them best equipped to try to approximate it in a society. Plato wasn't a fan of democracy, considering it the second-worst form of government after tyranny.

Although tyrants seem to enjoy a good life, Plato assures us that a tyrant 'never tastes of true freedom or friendship', as Julius Caesar learnt to his cost.

Another famous imaginary society is described by Thomas More in *Utopia* (1516). It's not clear whether More intended it as an ideal or just a satirical criticism of contemporary England. There is no private property in Utopia; all goods are held in warehouses and handed out to people who need them. Houses are identical and householders have to move every ten years to prevent people becoming too attached to one house. Each household has two slaves, who are either drawn from neighbouring countries or are Utopian criminals. Everyone dresses alike and must work on farms at regular intervals. People are required to learn a useful craft and all the able-bodied must work, men and women employed equally in all jobs. The ruling class of officials is made up of those who are identified at an early age as well-equipped to learn; these children are then specially educated. Officials only remain in post for as long as they are good at

'When several villages are united in a single complete community, large enough to be nearly or quite self-sufficing, the state comes into existence, originating in the bare needs of life, and continuing in existence for the sake of a good life. And, therefore, if the earlier forms of society are natural [i.e. the family and the village], so is the state, for it is the end of them, and the nature of a thing is its end. For what each thing is when fully developed, we call its nature, whether we are speaking of a man, a horse, or a family.'

Aristotle, *Politics*

THE IDEAL REPUBLIC

In Plato's ideal republic there is no discrimination between men and women, who are taught the same things and perform the same roles. There are no slaves; instead there is a social hierarchy (four estates or classes of people) and social mobility is minimal. Children are raised communally without knowledge of their parents, and adults are paired off for reproduction based on genetic criteria. This eradicates family ties that can lead to nepotism and forges strong ties of loyalty to the state and the communal 'good'. The young are taught only useful things – no poetry or other unnecessary art. The ruling classes are not allowed wealth as that can lead to corruption, but the producers may be rich or poor. The philosopher kings are chosen from the warrior class and subject to the most stringent restrictions. They are educated for 50 years before being called upon to rule.

their jobs. Gold is used to make chains for criminals and therefore it is not revered; jewels are worn by children and given up at adolescence.

> '**Life in More's Utopia, as in most others, would be intolerably dull. Diversity is essential to happiness, and in Utopia there is hardly any.**'
>
> Bertrand Russell, 1945

There have been plenty of subsequent fictitious city states that either genuinely propose an ideal form of government or satirize the authors' own inadequate society. In proposing how an ideal state should be governed, all beg the question – is a perfect society possible?

There are similarities between Thomas More's Utopia and communist states such as the USSR.

All together?

Both Plato and More took a collectivist approach – they focus on society as an organism in its own right, which is more than the sum of its constituent individuals. It would be nice to think that what is good for society as a whole also best serves individual citizens, but it seems not to be the case. There are probably few people who would like to live in a society where their partner is chosen for them on genetic grounds and their children taken away for communal rearing; where they can't choose the décor of their homes or the clothes they wear or the job they do. These strategies aim to reduce envy, discord and disruption and create a society that runs smoothly, provides sufficient for everyone's needs and is successful in itself. But it's not somewhere all of us would choose to live.

Today we set a lot more store by personal freedom and choice, and by expressing our individuality. Most people object to too much regulation by the state and liken it, pejoratively, to the over-regulated states of certain communist countries. Perhaps our view has changed because now, at least in the developed world, many of our basic needs are met. Our priorities have changed since Plato's time; we've become more demanding.

Why have a society at all?

If society is always in a state of tension between the requirements of the group and the requirements of the individual, why have it at all?

Aristotle believed that people naturally come together to form societies. We benefit from communal living, which gives us security, a wider variety of goods than we could gather alone, and the benefits of companionship. For this reason, we are willing to exchange some freedoms for the greater benefits offered by living in a society and entering into a 'social contract'.

The 17th-century English philosopher Thomas Hobbes took a darker view of humankind. He felt that if we didn't live in societies, it would be everyone for him- or herself and we would be perpetually fighting one another and doing nothing gainful. Society is preferable because it means we don't have to live constantly looking over our shoulders for someone approaching

'In such condition [i.e. natural man, outside society] there is no place for industry, because the fruit thereof is uncertain, and consequently, no culture of the earth, no navigation, nor the use of commodities that may be imported by sea, no commodious building, no instruments of moving and removing such things as require much force, no knowledge of the face of the earth, no account of time, no arts, no letters, no society, and which is worst of all, continual fear and danger of violent death, and the life of man, solitary, poor, nasty, brutish, and short.'

Thomas Hobbes,
Leviathan, 1651

with a club. We give up natural rights in exchange for a social contract which bound us to moral obligations that protect us.

Hobbes lists the laws of nature, although he says they can't really be called 'laws' as there is no one to enforce them. The first two are most significant:

(1) Every man must be considered to have a right to all things.
(2) Every man ought to be willing to give up that right if everyone else does the same.

The reason people will wish to join a commonwealth and choose to be ruled by another or others is 'the foresight of their own preservation, and of a more contented life'. Hobbes considered human desires to be so varied that attempting to build a society around trying to meet them was impossible. Instead he felt society could be built around avoiding the worst evil – violent death – as there would most likely be a consensus on this.

'Forced to be free'

The opposite view to Hobbes' is that humankind is more noble in the 'natural state' than in society. The 18th-century French philosopher Jean-Jacques Rousseau believed that the constraints of society bring out the worst in us. By entering into a social contract, we give up our innate, natural freedom. All existing societies (Rousseau meant those in the mid-18th century) enslave people without offering them the freedoms they deserve. In a just society, laws are written and enforced for the benefit of all, so by choosing to live in a society and accepting the social contract, we are freed. Indeed we are 'forced to be free' in that we are forced to follow the laws that free us. Rousseau denied that we have individual rights because, in the properly constituted state, they should not be needed.

Rousseau claimed that society, by introducing us to the idea of wanting things that other people have, leads us to be dissatisfied, envious, acquisitive and unhappy. We don't have these negative feelings in our 'natural' state.

The right to revolution

Occupying the middle ground between Hobbes and Rousseau, David Hume and John Locke argued that a social contract, and by extension a society, must guarantee individuals the right to own and control property. When people come together to form a society, there is necessarily some sort of 'sovereign', or leadership. The powers of the sovereign are limited by the right to own and control property. If the government violates that first principle, the people have a right to rise up and revolt, overthrowing the government so that the principles can be re-established.

Who chooses?

Most countries aren't in a position to choose a form of government starting from a blank slate, but if they were, the American philosopher John Rawls (1921–2002) had a solution. He proposed a theory known as Justice as Fairness, to protect

THE LEFT AND THE RIGHT

The opposing claims of the left and the right wing in politics reflect differing views of the role of society. The left wing leans towards public ownership and public provision, with a top-down approach to fixing society so that it works. The extreme is communism, with the 'means of production' owned by and operated for the benefit of the people. Right-wing policies favour private ownership and a non-interventionist, laissez-faire attitude to social engineering in the belief that the free market will eventually lead everything to resolve itself into an equilibrium that works. There is something of a Darwinian, evolutionary model of 'the survival of the fittest' to right-wing policies.

What responsibilities does a society have towards its poorest members? The assumption that market forces would eventually lead to equilibrium caused extreme hardship among the poor in Victorian London.

individual rights while promoting a fair allocation of resources. A new social order would be devised by people starting from what Rawls called the 'original position' and working behind a 'veil of ignorance': they have to design the justice system without knowing what their own position in society will be. They could end up as the ruler or as the lowliest worker or unemployed person.

CHAPTER 20

Are some people more equal than others?

We may believe in equality, but how many of us actually promote it?

What do we mean by equality?

Equality in a society can mean many things. It can signify equal rights, equality of opportunity or equal access to resources, for example. But where do human rights come from? And what type of rights or equality do we really have?

> 'Kindly remember that he whom you call your slave sprang from the same stock, is smiled upon by the same skies, and on equal terms with yourself breathes, lives, and dies.'
>
> Seneca, 1st century AD

The International Declaration of Human Rights sets out the kind of rights the modern world recognizes should be afforded to people:

- All human beings are born free and equal in dignity and rights. (Article 1)
- Everyone is entitled to all the rights and freedoms set forth in this Declaration, without distinction of any kind, such as race, colour, sex, language, religion, political or other opinion, national or social origin, property, birth or other status. (2)
- No one shall be subjected to torture or to cruel, inhuman or degrading treatment or punishment. (5)
- No one shall be subjected to arbitrary arrest, detention or exile. (9)
- Everyone, as a member of society, has the right to social security and is entitled to ... the economic, social and cultural rights indispensable for his dignity and the free development of his personality. (22)

> 'We hold these truths to be self-evident, that all men are created equal, [and] that they are endowed by their Creator with certain unalienable Rights, that among these are Life, Liberty and the pursuit of Happiness.'
>
> US Declaration of Independence, 1776

And so on.

Are we born free and equal?

Back in Ancient Greece, Aristotle noted that all people are *not* born equal. Some are born as slaves and born 'for' slavery, others are born to be masters. But this, as Jean-Jacques Rousseau noted later, is to confuse cause and effect. A person born into slavery and raised as a slave will naturally become a slave, but if taken from slavery and slave parents at the moment of birth, he or she would be no different from another person. No one is genetically a slave.

Aristotle's thinking on slavery was soon challenged. The Stoics proposed the essential equality in rights of all people: 'We are born for Justice, and that right is based, not upon one's opinions, but upon Nature.' (Cicero)

The idea that social position was not an innate characteristic of an individual and could not be fairly imposed on anyone, not even on those captured in war, was revolutionary.

Natural and inalienable rights

The idea that all people are born with natural and inalienable rights came to prominence during the Enlightenment. John Locke referred to the rights as 'life, liberty, and estate (property)' – a trio that was later enshrined in the US Declaration of Independence. Inalienable rights are those that cannot be surrendered or seized on entering into a social contract – the contract deemed to exist between citizen and government. The defence of slavery which claimed that slaves had surrendered their rights voluntarily was considered invalid because these natural rights could not be surrendered.

Other inalienable rights include the right to follow a faith and the right to one's own personality. Plenty of regimes have tried to strip away both of these. Persecution of different faiths has been common throughout history, and attempts to suppress personality were a mark of totalitarian states in the 20th century.

'Nonsense on stilts'

The idea that we have natural rights, or that there are natural laws, relies on us accepting there is something 'natural', 'right' or 'just' which exists 'out there'. It relies on the existence of universals, or possibly that of a God or an entity called Nature laying down rights and rules.

Jeremy Bentham, who called the idea of natural rights 'nonsense on stilts', claimed that rights could only be created by government or developed through tradition. There could be nothing inalienable about them as they have no special status. If they are not natural, they are also, then, culturally relative – they vary with time and place, and are different where there are different traditions and legal systems.

> '*It is a mistake to imagine that slavery pervades a man's whole being; the better part of him is exempt from it: the body indeed is subjected and in the power of a master, but the mind is independent, and indeed is so free and wild, that it cannot be restrained even by this prison of the body, wherein it is confined.*'
>
> Seneca the Younger, 1st century AD

> '*[All people have] certain inherent natural rights, of which they cannot, by any compact, deprive or divest their posterity.*'
>
> Virginia Declaration of Rights, 1776

Is might 'right'?

For Bentham, rights only emerge when people are interacting, or entering into a social contract. If we imagine Robinson Crusoe secluded on his island, does he have rights? Or are natural rights meaningless in his solitary state? When Friday turns up, does Robinson Crusoe have a 'right' to treat him as a servant? Does the Declaration of Human Rights touch him on his fictional island, giving him the right to own property? Does it give Friday the right to own any of the island?

Callicles, who lived in Athens 2,500 years ago, believed that the strongest among us will and should predominate and that

> 'Every man is responsible for his own faith, and he must see it for himself that he believes rightly. As little as another can go to hell or heaven for me, so little can he believe or disbelieve for me; and as little as he can open or shut heaven or hell for me, so little can he drive me to faith or unbelief. Since, then, belief or unbelief is a matter of every one's conscience, and since this is no lessening of the secular power, the latter should be content and attend to its own affairs and permit men to believe one thing or another, as they are able and willing, and constrain no one by force.'
>
> Martin Luther, 1523

this is the only 'natural' state. Social Darwinism takes the idea of the 'survival of the fittest' and applies it to society (though not in a way that Darwin intended) to justify the triumph of the strong over the weak. If people have 'certain unalienable rights', where do they come from? If they are bestowed by society, they are neither universal nor natural.

Natural inequality

A quick look at the mass of humanity shows that even if we are born with equal natural rights, we are not born with equal abilities. Some people are stronger or better-looking or cleverer or more musical than others. Our individual qualities and abilities are not equal and society values some above others.

Different cultures value different qualities. In the past, physical strength was a more valuable attribute than it is now that we

> 'Right is not the offspring of doctrine, but of power. All laws, commandments, or doctrines as to not doing to another what you do not wish done to you, have no inherent authority whatever, but receive it only from the club, the gallows, and the sword. A man truly free is under no obligation to obey any injunction, human or divine. Obedience is the sign of the degenerate. Disobedience is the stamp of the hero.'
>
> Leo Tolstoy's summary of the position presented by the Social Darwinist pamphlet *Might is Right*, 1890

don't have to fight off wild beasts or bring down prey for food. Some qualities which are valued may seem illogical: we pay professional sports players a lot of money; we value some actors, writers, painters and musicians highly. The fact that we are *not* all equal in natural abilities creates value, and value produces further types of inequality.

Equal opportunities?

A right to equal opportunities or equal treatment is not universally recognized but it is enshrined in some legal systems. It's hard to achieve, as all children start life from different positions and with different parents. Is it right for the rich to pay for better schooling for their children, giving them a clear, paid-for advantage not available to others?

From the 1920s to the 1970s, children in Israeli kibbutzim were raised communally, and spent only two or three hours a day with their parents. Nurit Leshem, who grew up on a kibbutz, says, 'We were educated to be the same; but we were, for all that, different.'

What's opportunity and how equal can it be?

It's difficult to define equality of opportunity. Equal opportunity to realize our personal potential will require unequal provision – the musical child will benefit from music lessons which might not benefit the child who excels at sport.

As with any problem relating to existing societies, we are not starting from a level playing field. Some people have natural advantages by virtue of birth and some might have disadvantages for historical reasons. One answer to this is positive discrimination, or what Rawls calls 'fair equality of opportunity' to try to compensate for disadvantage. It's a controversial measure that raises objections – not least that it does exactly what it is meant to oppose – because it favours one person over another on grounds of birth, ethnicity, gender, and so on.

> '**Every member of the commonwealth must be permitted to attain any degree of status . . . to which his talent, his industry, and his luck might bring him; and his fellow subjects may not block his way [because of] hereditary prerogatives.'**
>
> Immanuel Kant

Political philosopher Robert Nozick (1938–2002) and economist Milton Friedman (1912–2006) opposed equal opportunity measures because they saw them restricting the right of others to employ whoever they chose and using their own property as they saw fit.

Some are more equal than others

In his novel *Animal Farm*, George Orwell satirized the USSR under Stalin and Lenin, showing how a revolution that sought to make everyone equal quickly led to a repressive society in which some people starved while others prospered.

Economists have found it impossible to create or even model a society in which horizontal inequality – inequality between people of equivalent abilities at equal starting points – does not emerge. Robert Nozick gave an example of how inequality emerges. (He used it to argue against trying to impose equality of wealth.) Suppose society begins with everyone owning $100 (£60). A sportsman – the basketball player Wilt Chamberlain in his example – says he will only play in public if everyone who wants to watch pays 25 cents. By the end of the season, the sportsman has $250,000 (£150,000) because many people wanted to watch him play. They have freely given their 25 cents. Why should we take any of it away from him? Equality of opportunity involves equal opportunities to succeed or fail, to become rich or poor, making it inherently incompatible with equality of outcome. Which would we prefer? Right-wing politics leans towards equality of opportunity and left-wing politics leans towards equality of outcome.

In a society otherwise intent on treating all citizens alike, the USSR had programmes to identify and nurture talent in sport and music – but for the glory of the state rather than self-realization of the individual.

Many people in the economically developed world support equality of opportunity, yet want to limit the influx of immigrants. We legislate for the fair treatment of employees in our own lands, yet buy cheap goods made by workers in appalling conditions overseas. We say men and women have equal rights, and that people of different ethnic backgrounds have equal rights, yet women earn less on average than men, and black people earn less than white people and are more likely to go to jail. Do we really mean all people are born equal, or just 'people like us'?

Should we rob one Peter to pay several Pauls?

How do we balance the rights of the individual against those of the many?

In 2013, the Cypriot economy was in a dire state. In an unprecedented and unpopular move, the Cypriot government decided to seize up to 60 per cent of bank deposits over 100,000 euros (£82,000, $138,000). The move particularly targeted Russian oligarchs who were using Cyprus as a tax haven, but it inevitably affected some ordinary citizens of Cyprus. The government believed that, in taking money from the richest investors, it could potentially save a larger number of poorer Cypriots from greater hardship if the currency and banking sector collapsed. Does that make the action right?

The greatest good for the greatest number

The Cypriot cash-snatch can be defended using the principle of Utilitarianism, based on the premise that actions are morally good or bad according to how far they maximize happiness and minimize pain. The actions that bring the greatest benefit to the largest number of people are chosen over alternatives. 'Happiness' is taken to mean pleasure and freedom from pain. Pleasure is not just wine, (wo)men and song, but includes higher intellectual pleasures.

Utilitarianism is unselfish and egalitarian – perhaps to a fault. Everyone's happiness counts equally, so sometimes utilitarianism will require personal sacrifice. Most moral and legal codes, and even just good manners, are built at least approximately on a Utilitarian basis. It's generally best if we ban stealing, then we can all be fairly confident that we can reap the fruits of our labour. Otherwise we'd spend a lot of time looking over our shoulders to see who's creeping up with the intention of pinching our kebab or tablet computer. On the whole, Utilitarianism seems to work reasonably well.

> '*Actions are right in proportion as they tend to promote happiness, wrong as they tend to produce the reverse of happiness.*'
>
> John Stuart Mill, 1863

> 'Pleasure, and freedom from pain, are the only things desirable as ends . . . all desirable things are desirable either for the pleasure inherent in themselves, or as means to the promotion of pleasure and the prevention of pain.'
>
> John Stuart Mill

THE 'FELICIFIC CALCULUS'

It's not always obvious which course of action will produce the greatest good. Jeremy Bentham (1748–1832), the originator of classic Utilitarianism, produced a 'felicific calculus' to help work out tricky problems of Utilitarian morality. This takes account of each pleasure and pain produced by an action and rates it for six qualities:

- Intensity
- Duration
- Certainty or uncertainty: how likely or unlikely is it to occur?
- Propinquity or remoteness: how soon will it occur?
- Fecundity: how likely is it to produce more sensations of the same kind?
- Purity: how likely is it to produce more sensations of the opposite kind?

The total points for pleasure and pain must then be multiplied by the number of people who will be affected in each way. If the final calculation shows a balance of pleasure, the act is approved. If it shows a balance of pain, the act is deemed a bad idea.

People as trading tokens

There are logical objections to Utilitarianism. One is that it seems inhumane, trading in human happiness as though it were a commodity in an economy. It would seem to condone the abuse of the few by the many. If 100,000 Romans enjoy watching a slave torn apart by lions in the Coliseum, is the enjoyment of the audience enough to outweigh the agony of the slave? We could say the slave's suffering is so immense that it outweighs the pleasure of the happy spectators. Or we could say that the spectators are not enjoying true happiness, and the degradation involved in watching such an event would be more properly termed a pain than a pleasure.

But there are other cases in which the common-sense answer to a question and the Utilitarian answer are at odds.

Jeremy Bentham was, at his own request, made into an auto-icon after his death. His body was dissected, then the skeleton padded with straw and dressed. The head of the icon is a wax copy, as his real head looks rather ghoulish (between his feet) and is not usually displayed. Bentham occasionally sits in on meetings at University College London where he is marked as 'present but not voting'.

There are circumstances in which personal feelings might prevent someone doing the 'right' thing. Imagine you are held hostage with ten other people. The hostage-takers want to kill one particular person but can't identify that person. You know who it is. If no one identifies the target, half the hostages will be killed. If you identify the person, they will just kill him/her.

Would you identify the person? What if you were the person? What if your child or partner was the person?

Utilitarianism would demand that you reveal the one person to save five. But your conscience, emotional involvement and self-interest are all likely to affect your decision. One problem with Utilitarianism is that it requires us to act according to clinical, mathematical logic – and people are seldom like that.

Peters and Pauls

All economic systems try to find a balance between taking money from rich people and giving it to poorer people. Aiming for the greatest good to the greatest number is an effective way of staying in power. In a democracy, people will not vote for a government that gets the balance wrong. In the worst case, the people will rise up to overthrow a government which gets it very wrong. But if most people are happy, the government is likely to be stable.

THOUGHT EXPERIMENT: THE INHOSPITABLE HOSPITAL

Suppose five patients in a hospital all need vital organ transplants in order to live. A patient who is not critically ill comes in for a routine operation. The surgeon could kill the patient, make it look like a freak misfortune, and use his organs to save five other people. Is it immoral to kill one person to save five? Or should the surgeon heal the healthy patient and let the others die? Common sense tells us the surgeon should not kill the healthy patient. If asked why, most people would say that the deaths of the five people would be random misfortune, but deliberately killing one healthy person would be murder. They might say that the surgeon doesn't have the right to decide who should live or die. But isn't he deciding anyway, as soon as the options are clear to him?

Negotiating with hijackers requires balancing currently endangered lives against the possible future consequence of more hijackings.

The general perception of the banking crisis which started in 2007 is that greed on the part of a small number of people caused misery to a large number of poorer people. The 99 per cent movement claims to represent 99 per cent of society – the portion which did not profit from the banking boom years. The use of the figure taps into people's natural utilitarian tendency to believe that the greatest benefit to the greatest number is the best way to calculate the morality of an act.

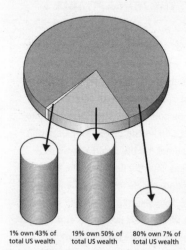

1% own 43% of
total US wealth

19% own 50% of
total US wealth

80% own 7% of
total US wealth

In 2007, just before the financial crash, the top 1 per cent of the US population owned 43 per cent of the wealth. The bottom 80 per cent owned only 7 per cent of the wealth.

CHAPTER 22

How do you define a virtuous life?

Is it possible always to do as you would be done by?

The principle of the Golden Rule is that we should treat everyone the way we would like to be treated (see Chapter 16).

Living virtuously

People who try to live the purest, most virtuous lives are few and far between. One way of doing this is to spend your life in the service of others or at least interacting honestly with them. Another way is to eschew the trappings of normal life and seek a form of enlightenment or tranquillity through contemplation or prayer. To date, no philosopher seems to have taken an approach which involves owning four houses, a string of polo ponies and a yacht.

> *'It is easier for a camel to go through the eye of a needle, than for a rich man to enter into the kingdom of God.'*
>
> King James Bible,
> Matthew, 19:23

The selfless life

The Greek philosopher Diogenes (400–325BC) took the eschewing of material possessions to an extreme. The ultimate ascetic, he set up home in a large pot in the marketplace and owned as little as he could. He had a few rags and a drinking bowl. At least he had a drinking bowl to start with, but when he saw a young boy drinking from his cupped hands he realized that the bowl was a luxury he could do without and dashed it to the ground. He didn't earn any money as that would clearly be buying into the materialism he despised, but lived on food he was given or that he found. Diogenes taught that the way to happiness was by living 'according to nature' – satisfying the body's most basic needs as simply as possible and shunning all possessions, personal ties and attachments. He demanded that his followers deliberately lay themselves open to scorn and ridicule as a practice in detachment.

Immanuel Kant's categorical imperative states that you should act towards other people as you would want all other

Living in a jar, Diogenes shunned all material possessions to achieve personal enlightenment.

people to act towards you. This theory was immortalized by the character of Mrs Doasyouwouldbedoneby in Charles Kingsley's *The Water Babies* (see page 171). Kant's moral asceticism states that the rightness or wrongness of our actions does not depend on their consequences but on whether they fulfil our duty. It is not up to us to decide whether a particular way of behaving is 'right' or moral – this assessment can only be reached through the use of practical reason. Virtue, said Kant, needs to 'muster all its forces to overcome the obstacles it must contend with ... [and] ... sacrifice many of the joys of life.' It's not all gloom, however, as he goes on to say that virtue consists in 'a cheerful frame of mind', a strong sense of one's inner worth and a 'consciousness of one's restored freedom'.

> '*Act only according to that maxim whereby you can, at the same time, will that it should become a universal law.*'
>
> Immanuel Kant, 1785

POLE DANCING, SYRIAN STYLE

The Stylites were early Christian ascetics who lived on top of columns or poles in the desert. The trendsetter was probably Simeon Stylites, who climbed his pillar in Syria in 423 and stayed there until his death 37 years later. There were variants. Theodoret of Cyrus, a contemporary of Simeon of Stylites, wrote of a hermit he had seen who lived for ten years in a tub suspended from poles, and St Alypius is reported to have built a pillar and lived on it for 67 years. For the first 53 years he was standing up, but when his feet could no longer take the strain he lay down. Incredibly, he is said to have lived to the age of 118.

To find the tranquillity he needed for his devotions, St Simeon Stylites spent 37 years living on top of a pillar.

A trade-off

Medieval Europe saw many wandering friars and monks who lived on charitable donations and in return prayed for the souls of the society that provided for them. They traded prayer and wisdom, which people considered valuable commodities, for food and other necessities. Each person who gave to a friar did so of his or her own volition, and no doubt felt that their act of charity was ennobling or buying them some remission.

Kant's imperative is usually applied to lifestyles which seem selfish. Society would collapse if everyone lived like a billionaire; we have recent evidence of this in the financial crisis that followed the banking disasters of 2008. Too many people were living beyond their means, in a way that neither their income nor society's productivity could support.

Many systems are based on the premise that the majority of people will do the 'right' or moral thing. They range from social security benefit systems, which work as long as the majority pay in and those who take out are in genuine need, to national vaccination programmes that control dangerous diseases by creating 'herd immunity'. But in every society there is a critical balance, which is why the needs of the individual are generally subordinate to the well-being of the many – the greater good.

The effectiveness of vaccination is dependent on herd immunity. Opting out of vaccination means that the many are potentially put at risk by the few.

MMR: A PRACTICAL LESSON IN THE CATEGORICAL IMPERATIVE

In 1998, a fraudulent paper published in the medical journal *The Lancet* claimed that the triple MMR vaccine to protect children against measles, mumps and rubella could lead to autism. As a result, the number of parents having their children vaccinated dropped. By 2008, measles was once more endemic (circulating in the general population) in the UK, following a steady decline in cases during the previous 14 years. This was a direct result of the drop-off in vaccination. The diseases that MMR protects against can cause lasting damage or death in children.

When enough people are vaccinated, the few who are not are protected by 'herd immunity' – the immunity of the majority which makes it very difficult for a disease to circulate. When insufficient people are vaccinated, all unvaccinated people become vulnerable. Do parents have the moral right to depend on herd immunity (the result of the dutiful actions of others) rather than accept the tiny risk they think the vaccine presents?

The vaccine was subsequently proven not to cause autism, but the loss of herd immunity led to many cases of sickness and four deaths in the UK.

CHAPTER 23

Can a robot think for itself?

What are the limits of artificial intelligence?

Science fiction films and novels often depict a world taken over by artificially intelligent robots, who then proceed to destroy human beings. Is there a chance it might happen? And should we allow a state of affairs in which it could happen?

Primal fear?

The word 'robot' was first used in a 1920 play *R.U.R.* by Czech writer Karel Čapek, in which a race of self-replicating robots, originally constructed as slaves, rebel against their masters and try to destroy humanity. So the fear of the robots taking over is as old as robots themselves. Unlikely as it may seem, is it a possibility? Active rebellion requires artificial intelligence (AI) – some reasoning or learning that goes beyond simple programming.

THE THREE LAWS OF ROBOTICS

Science fiction writer Isaac Asimov set out the three laws of robotics in his short story 'Runaround', published in 1942:

1. A robot may not injure a human or, through inaction, allow a human to come to harm.
2. A robot must obey the orders given to it by humans, except where such orders would conflict with the First Law.
3. A robot must protect its own existence as long as such protection does not conflict with the First or Second Law.

Later, Asimov added a 'zeroth' law:

0. A robot may not harm humanity or, by inaction, allow humanity to come to harm.

The singularity

In 1993, mathematician Vernor Vinge proposed an event called the 'singularity' – the point at which AI exceeds human capabilities and can design ever better and more powerful versions of itself, quickly leading to intelligence far beyond our understanding. At this point, Vinge said, 'the human era will be ended'. The singularity is the starting point for sci-fi writers who postulate that machines are taking over, destroying us, using us as slaves or even producing a paradise for us to live in. As they are more intelligent than anything we can conceive of, we can't anticipate what they will do. The best prediction, or best wild-stab-in-the-dark, for when this might come about is 2025–45, based on trends in developing computer capabilities.

'There is no security against the ultimate development of mechanical consciousness, in the fact of machines possessing little consciousness now. A mollusc has not much consciousness. Reflect upon the extraordinary advance which machines have made during the last few hundred years, and note how slowly the animal and vegetable kingdoms are advancing. The more highly organized machines are creatures not so much of yesterday, as of the last five minutes, so to speak, in comparison with past time.'

Samuel Butler, *Erewhon*, 1872

What is intelligence?

There is no universally accepted definition of intelligence so it's hard to say exactly what we mean by AI. Most people would say it's not simply the ability to work things out by following rules – computers are already much better at that than we are. Intelligence seems to involve an ability to learn, to form creative leaps and forge links or see connections that are not obvious. Human intelligence produces jokes and metaphors, interprets and uses nuance, interprets context, and picks up clues from the behaviour of others.

BANNED AI

As well as sci-fi scenarios in which the robots have taken over, there are those in which AI has been banned or defeated. The Butlerian Jihad occurs in the backstory of Frank Herbert's *Dune* novels, which are set in the distant future. In a revolt occurring 10,000 years before the events of *Dune* (published in 1965), certain technologies, including AI and computers, are prohibited and their reinvention is banned with the commandment 'Thou shalt not make a machine in the likeness of a human mind.'

In theory, an AI doctor-robot could make more accurate and speedier diagnoses than a human doctor. It could store the details of millions of medical conditions, correlate their symptoms and recommend a treatment.

But humans have something unique to offer (at the moment, that is). By using his or her intuition and experience, a human doctor may be able to tell if a patient who is presenting with stomach-ache has an underlying condition (depression, for example) which they are too embarrassed or afraid to talk about. A computer might not pick that up.

How close are we?

Depending on who you ask, we either have genuinely intelligent and conscious computers already, or we are years away from achieving them.

Neurologists point to the complexity of animal brains and say that computers are not yet able to emulate anything but the simplest of organisms. The whole of the internet is not as complex as the connections within a single human brain – and that's not to mention all the other things the brain can do. Computer scientists point to the ways in which they are modelling neurons and beginning to build 'brains' in a modular way, emulating the structure of real (but not necessarily human) brains and nervous systems. Some AI developers suggest it is not in fact necessary to mimic the human brain in order to produce intelligence.

THE TURING TEST

Computer pioneer Alan Turing (1912–54) proposed a test to determine whether AI had been achieved and whether a computer could be said to think like a human being. A computer passes the Turing test if a human interrogator can't tell it apart from another human in conversation. Turing believed it might be better to emulate the mind of a child and to educate this child-computer than to try to build a computer like an adult brain.

One objection to Turing's criterion is its demand that machine intelligence is very similar to human intelligence. As Stuart Russell and Peter Norvig have pointed out in their textbook *Artificial Intelligence: A Modern Approach* (1995), we don't demand that an aeroplane flies well enough to fool birds before we accept that it can fly. In fact it was only when we gave up trying to copy how birds fly that we succeeded in making working planes.

But would it be a brain?

Philosophers disagree about whether, if we could make an electronic replica of the human brain or an intelligent non-replica, it would 'count' as a brain or as intelligent even if it could apparently perform the same functions.

> '*If a machine behaves as intelligently as a human being, then it is as intelligent as a human being.*'
>
> Alan Turing

In 1980, the American philosopher John Searle suggested a thought experiment that he called the 'Chinese room' to explain how AI does not have understanding. Imagine a person in a closed room who is passed questions written in Chinese. The person doesn't understand Chinese, but has a big book in which he can look up the questions and find suitable answers. He passes his answers back, and everyone outside the room thinks he appears to understand Chinese. In a similar way, AI could perform as though it had understanding, without actually having it. Searle distinguished between what he called weak AI and strong AI:

- Weak AI – 'A physical symbol system [effectively, a computer] can act intelligently'
- Strong AI – 'A physical symbol system can have a mind and mental states'

Strong AI is the version that concerns philosophers.

Early AI developers assumed that the mind processes information in chunks according to certain rules and they believed this mechanism could be replicated by a machine. But unconscious instincts are key to human intelligence and expertise, and these can't be reproduced by a set of rules or algorithms which a computer could follow – hence the limitations of the AI doctor. The American philosopher and academic Hubert Dreyfus, addressing this limitation of AI, said that true human intelligence and expertise is not 'knowing-that' (factual knowledge) but is 'knowing-how' (knowledge in action, as it were).

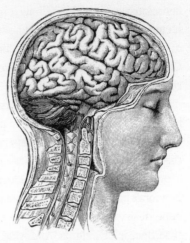

Brainbox: in 2005, a computer model of the human brain, with 10^{11} neurons, took 50 days to do the equivalent of one second's 'brain activity'.

PHILOSOPHICAL ZOMBIES

The question of whether a machine can have a mind is a version of the 'problem of other minds', which asks whether we can be certain anything or anyone else has a mind. How would you feel if you discovered you are the only minded being in existence and everyone else is a flesh automaton, or philosophical zombie?

Turing observed that human intuitions might well follow rules – they just could be rules we haven't observed yet. In this case, human instincts might at some point be emulated by machine intelligence. Since Dreyfus' work in the 1970s, research in AI has moved towards neural networks and evolutionary algorithms designed to deal specifically with the kind of unconscious processing, contexts and links not emulated in the early models.

From thingness to being

It's one thing to be intelligent, but a completely different thing to be conscious. Again, there's no consensus about what consciousness is or where/how it is located. John Searle suggests it emerges from a collection of neurons, just as the property of wetness emerges from a collection of water molecules (see Chapter 6). In that case, an intelligent machine would also be a conscious machine.

Can we conceive of types of consciousness that are not like human consciousness? American philosopher Daniel Dennett claims that machines are already conscious, and even a thermostat is 'conscious'. It's not a view shared by many.

But if a machine has a consciousness it opens up a whole new Pandora's box of dilemmas. Could a conscious machine feel hope, despair, pain, anger, love, curiosity, envy, longing, pride? If so, does it have rights? And what responsibilities do we have towards such a machine? – or should that be 'such a being'? These questions have been explored in great detail in science-fiction writing and films.

How much power to give the machines?

There are many ways in which we have made ourselves vulnerable by relying heavily on technology. The banking crisis that began in 2007–8 was caused largely by runaway computer algorithms. The Black–Scholes mathematical equation at the heart of the financial market had been used inappropriately to allow trading in derivatives (not a real product, just hypothetical money and prospects of profit) to reach a value of a quadrillion dollars a year. That's ten times the value of all actual stuff produced in the whole world over a century. As computers make decisions in a fraction of a second, things can spiral out of control very, very quickly. Hand-in-hand with computers giving us the capability to make and do more, we have the chance that they will destroy more – and they don't even need to develop a malevolent intelligence to do it.

ROBOTS IN LOVE

In the film *AI* (2001), directed by Steven Spielberg, a young boy android called David is programmed to display love. When his 'imprinting protocol' is initiated, David develops a strong bond with the woman to whom he is a substitute son. This love can never be undone, and he still loves her after humans have become extinct, 2,000 years later. What duties would we have towards robots that could love us?

In Japan, the government is offering 50–60 per cent subsidies for research and development to companies developing care robots for elderly people. Japan suffers from a serious shortage of care workers, and robots might fill the gap. How should we feel about people becoming dependent on and perhaps emotionally attached to robots?

The killer robots are here

The use of drones – unmanned, computerized vehicles and weapons – in warfare is highly contentious. Members of the armed forces argue that the lives of many soldiers are saved by the deployment of drones in perilous missions over or into enemy territory. But the argument against their use is that we are allowing technology to make the 'decision' to kill humans. Whether it really is a decision is debatable – the drone follows instructions to seek, identify and deal with a target.

The case for drones is largely utilitarian – it achieves the end of destroying a particular target (usually an insurgent hidden deep within enemy territory) and of minimizing the collateral damage. But there is what philosophers call a 'fact-value' confusion here. The fact that it *is* easy to kill targets using drones doesn't mean that we *should* do it.

The case against drones addresses the utilitarian points and takes a moral stance. It points out that there have been accidental killings, and that it's not valid to argue *for* something on the basis of it being better than an alternative (such as wide-scale bombing) which was never proposed. It questions whether it is ever acceptable to use a method of killing so dissociated from human engagement, which resembles something that can be done with a 'PlayStation mentality'.

CAN WE LIMIT KNOWLEDGE?

Knowledge can bring benefits and dangers. Ever since the biblical Fall of Man, knowledge has been linked with danger. Knowledge of sub-atomic physics made nuclear weapons possible, but it also gave us the medical benefits of technologies such as MRI and CAT scans. Knowledge of the genome helps us improve crops and cure disease but could also give a terrorist the ability to release a killer virus. Are there some types of knowledge that are just too dangerous to pursue? Should we limit research in some areas because of the potential for disaster, just as we limit it for ethical reasons? Or will that render us powerless if an evil genius gets there ahead of us?

Using drones can also be damaging psychologically and spiritually. A report released by the Pentagon in 2011 revealed that 30 per cent of drone operators suffered burn-out as a result of 'existential crisis'. Pilots can also be adversely affected in the opposite way, with killing becoming 'normalized'. The use of drones is cloaked in secrecy – the targets chosen by top-level politicians and military leaders – and this lack of transparency might be a political and philosophical problem. Some philosophers argue, however, that ethics don't apply in the arena of war (see Chapter 18).

CHAPTER 24

Are we being watched?

Governments claim that surveillance keeps us safe from harm. But what is the cost to our privacy?

There are few places we can go in our towns and cities where there is not a CCTV camera peering at us. If you include surveillance by government of our emails, phone calls, texts and web activity, it can feel as if little of our lives is private. Is mass surveillance good or bad? Is it useful? How can we balance the protection of the public with privacy of the individual?

You're on film

CCTV cameras serve two distinct purposes: deterrence and detection. They record activity in an area, providing possible evidence that can help with police investigations if a crime is committed. They also deter people from committing a crime where the cameras can record it – why do something if you know you'll be in trouble for it?

Now you see it, now you don't

Are there crimes you would commit if you thought you could get away with them? Maybe not big crimes, but little ones, like using an 'access only' road as a shortcut?

If there were a policeman standing at the end of the access-only road, few people would drive down it for fear of getting into trouble. It's unlikely there will be a policeman present

Whether CCTV cameras actually do reduce crime is disputed.

every day, however. The next time the policeman is away, people will use the shortcut again. Now suppose that instead of standing still, the policeman was obviously walking up and down the road. Next time it looks as though there is no policeman, but no one can be sure. Maybe he's just further down the street. Perhaps there will still be trouble if you drive down there. So you take another route.

The conclusion is counter-intuitive: the *possible* presence of a policeman is at least as good a deterrent, and possibly a better one, as the *definite* presence of a policeman.

In the latter case, if the policeman isn't visible, he has no deterrent effect. A hard-pressed local authority could use the walking policeman to act as a deterrent on several roads because he doesn't have to be visible on any one of them to still have an impact.

Look out – they're all around you

The principle of the policeman who might or might not be there lies behind an experimental design for prisons proposed in the late 18th century by the English philosopher Jeremy Bentham. The 'panopticon' is a circular structure, with each prisoner housed in a cell facing in towards a central observation tower. A guard sits in the tower, in a room with windows all around but with blinds obscuring the room from outside observers. The guard can see into any of the surrounding cells, but no one in a cell can see into the watchtower. The effect, according to Bentham, is that the prisoners will never know when they are being observed, so will be self-policing, acting always as though they are being observed. A warren-like network of passages would allow guards to enter and leave the watchtower unobserved, so there doesn't need to be a guard present all the time – the deterrent effect of the potential guard will be as great as if there is someone watching all the time.

Bentham advertised the panopticon as 'a new mode of obtaining power of mind over mind, in a quantity hitherto without example', which sounds gleefully oppressive. But he didn't intend his design to be used as a means of oppression. He was in favour of individualism and promoted freedom of expression, equal rights for women, the right to divorce, the abolition of slavery and of the

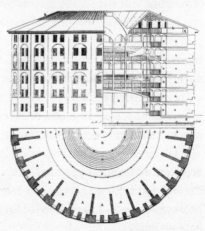

death penalty, and the decriminalization of homosexuality – all pretty radical aims for the late 1700s. He called the panopticon 'a mill for grinding rogues honest' – in other words, a system for reforming and re-educating criminals.

Nevertheless, the French philosopher Michel Foucault saw the panopticon as an icon of disciplinary power and the pervasive and invasive impulse to observe, and that is how it is generally considered.

> '*Morals reformed – health preserved – industry invigorated – instruction diffused – public burthens lightened . . . all by a simple idea in Architecture!*'
>
> Jeremy Bentham

Can you 'grind rogues honest'?

The prisoners in the panopticon might behave themselves, but surely only because they think they are being watched and fear punishment if they misbehave? This is not really making them honest, it is only making them obedient. Bentham might have argued that by always doing the right thing, the prisoners become accustomed to good behaviour and it becomes their default setting, as it were. Good behaviour becomes ingrained and automatic, so they are reformed.

If you simply want a society of law-abiding citizens, perhaps automatic obedience is good enough. But Kant would disagree. Although in favour of people obeying the moral law because it was the law, he wanted them to obey it because they *chose* to – because they were guided by their conscience.

Unthinking obedience is not the mark of a moral person. Indeed, constant surveillance and

> '*He who is subjected to a field of visibility, and who knows it, assumes responsibility for the constraints of power; he makes them play spontaneously upon himself; he inscribes in himself the power relation in which he simultaneously plays both roles; he becomes the principle of his own subjection.*'
>
> Michel Foucault, 1975

VIRTUAL PANOPTICON

'*There was of course no way of knowing whether you were being watched at any given moment . . . you had to live . . . in the assumption that every sound you made was overheard, and, except in darkness, every movement scrutinized.*'

In George Orwell's novel *Nineteen Eighty-Four* (1949), the population is subject to constant surveillance through 'telescreens' installed in all homes and public places.

fear of the consequences of our behaviour could ultimately be damaging for society. Surveillance stunts our growth as responsible individuals; we become morally flabby because we are not exercising our judgement or reflecting on our behaviour or challenging our actions and the rules by which we live. Although Bentham believed it would produce obedient citizens, simply internalizing the rules produces what Foucault described as individuals who are responsible for their own subjugation.

'If you're not guilty, you have nothing to hide'

In 2013, the American computer specialist Edward Snowden revealed the wide-ranging surveillance of ordinary citizens through their online activity by authorities in the USA, the UK

Unthinking obedience to authority can have terrible consequences. In a healthy society, citizens take responsibility for their moral choices and challenge injustices. The targeting of minorities and the setting up of concentration camps are symptoms of a sickness at the heart of society.

and Israel. Snowden uncovered intrusion on an unprecedented scale, and more information soon emerged – including allegations that the USA had spied on major European political figures including the German Chancellor and the Pope. Wanted for espionage and theft of government property, Snowden fled the USA.

The case reopened a long-running debate about privacy and security. On one side, the authorities who want to observe the public claim that if you have nothing to hide, you shouldn't be worried about being observed. On the other side, people who object to being observed say that if they are not doing anything wrong they have a right to privacy. The public is divided into those who are comforted by security measures and those who are affronted by them.

Justifying surveillance

The American philosopher Emrys Westacott has suggested that the morality of surveillance is determined by:

- whether there is a justified cause
- the means used
- whether the surveillance and degree of intrusion is in proportion to the risk that surveillance is supposed to guard against

SHOULD YOU FILTER THE INTERNET FOR YOUR CHILDREN?

There is a lot of concern about online content which is unsuitable for children. Some parents use filtering software to prevent their children accessing violent or sexual content, either accidentally or on purpose. The danger of the child being upset or damaged by what they see must be set against the need for the child to develop self-regulating behaviour. For many people, it means the online activity of younger children will be monitored and regulated, but the restrictions and protections should decrease as children grow and learn to take responsibility for themselves.

In addition to these factors, the watched citizen worries about the security and accuracy of the information collected and whether it might be misused. It looks as though all the cards are in the hands of the authorities, but that's not entirely the case. In a democracy, governments have to retain the trust of the people in order to stay in power. People who are not trusted and respected don't give their trust and respect in return.

In assessing whether they feel surveillance is justified, and whether they are willing to tolerate the invasion of their privacy, people will think first about who is being protected.

Some people object to increased security checks at airports; others find them reassuring.

We are most tolerant of surveillance if we believe it is for our own protection. The authorities in the USA and UK insist that the increased level of surveillance makes people's lives safer. Sometimes the surveillance is intended to protect the government, or individuals in a government. In this case, the population is least likely to be sympathetic to the erosion of privacy as it does not seem to be a fair trade – the public gets little benefit from the loss of privacy.

> '**You can't have 100 per cent security, and also then have 100 per cent privacy and zero inconvenience.**'
> US President Barack Obama, 2013

Some commentators have challenged the view that it has to be a choice between privacy and security. They have asked for security measures which do not invade privacy.

Just a number

For some people, the role of technology in the surveillance of private communications makes the whole issue more sinister. When people are treated as data, they feel affronted, undervalued and stripped of human dignity. With plenty of experience of human/computer error in other areas, many of us fear the harm that could be done by a miscalculation or a wrong algorithm. Surveillance then becomes not just about the erosion of privacy, but about the erosion of power and even of our sense of personhood and the value of that personhood.

Should you rock the boat?

Is it sometimes useful to rebel?

Many people will do almost anything for an easy life, and find it hard to deal with a person whose ideas are outside the mainstream. 'Don't rock the boat', we're told if we ask an awkward question. 'Go with the crowd.' 'Sixty million (or a hundred million, or a billion) people can't be wrong.'

Can't they?

A brief history of being wrong

Humanity only progresses when people find a better way of doing things, or a better model or theory. Long ago, we all thought the Sun went around the Earth. We used the highly toxic metal mercury to treat syphilis. People kept slaves and women and children were regarded as 'lesser' beings. Pandas were thought to be mythical. And what about all the people who have believed (and still believe) in completely different sets of gods through the ages? They can't all have been right. The quantity of people who hold a belief is no guarantee that the belief is true.

Leaps and bounds

The American historian, physicist and philosopher of science Thomas Kuhn (1922–96) suggested that science goes through long periods during which no one challenges the prevailing models; it then undergoes brief periods of radical change or paradigm shift. Most of the time, no one deviates far from standard thinking. It is only when someone thinks 'outside the box' that significant progress is made. Often the people who make these big leaps of imagination are disbelieved and ridiculed to start with – such is the power of popular opinion.

In 1543, the astronomer Mikolaj Kopernik (Copernicus) published his theory that the Earth goes around the Sun. More than 70 years later, the Roman Catholic Church decided that the idea was 'foolish and absurd ... and formally heretical', and demanded that the astronomer Galileo stop teaching it. The geocentric model was so widely accepted before Copernicus that it had the status of consensus reality – it was effectively real by virtue of being so widely believed.

Die rather than lie

The Greek philosopher Socrates made himself very unpopular by questioning the citizens of Athens about their beliefs and ideas. He would stop people in the marketplace and challenge them to define concepts such as virtue or justice. He quickly showed them that their unconsidered, received opinions didn't really work. He was soon in trouble for corrupting the youth of Athens (his students) and for being an irritant. The city's elite told him he had to stop teaching philosophy. Socrates refused, saying he would rather die a thousand times over than refrain from telling the truth. He was tried for moral corruption and impiety, convicted and instructed to take his own life by drinking poison.

> '*Have the courage to go against the tide.*'
>
> Pope Francis, 2013

Rather than going with the flow of received wisdom, Socrates chose to end his life by drinking hemlock.

THE RITE OF SPRING

The Rite of Spring is a ballet and orchestral piece by Ivor Stravinsky, produced for Sergei Diaghilev's Ballets Russes and premiered in Paris in 1913. The avant-garde nature of the work was so startling that it caused a near riot in the audience. Now it is considered one of the most significant musical works of the 20th century.

An easy life

We're all brought up with certain beliefs. If it occurs to us that they could be wrong, we might or might not challenge them; but most of us tend to believe that if lots of people agree on something, their numbers prove they are almost certainly right. And, importantly, most people prefer to go with the crowd and be liked, rather than run the risk of being ridiculed and hated.

Socrates recommended that, instead of just taking on board all the ideas that are current and unquestioned in society, we should hold each one up to scrutiny and decide, through investigation and logical thought, whether we really believe it to be true or just. He considered that blindly to hold and defend an opinion you have not thought about is to squander the main benefit of being human.

> *'The unexamined life is not worth living.'*
>
> Socrates

Against the tide

As children, most of us live in fear of being labelled as a snitch – someone who gets others into trouble by 'grassing' on them to teachers or parents. Who broke the window? Who let the class hamster out? Who wrote rude words on the board? It's considered to be fraternizing with the enemy (grown-ups) to uncover the culprit. As a consequence, the snitch (or whistle-blower, depending on your point of view) may be scorned and bullied for their pains.

This attitude persists into adulthood. It's formalized in the criminal world, where a grass can expect a nasty fate. How many of us have frowned on criminal behaviour but not had the courage to report it?

Going along with what other people tell you to think can have disastrous consequences.

A whistle-blower exposes corruption, malpractice or dodgy dealing in an organization, in the public interest. Like their childhood equivalents, whistle-blowers are often reviled, persecuted and can suffer dire consequences for their public-spirited actions. Although many countries have laws to protect whistle-blowers, it's often the case that those who do report wrong-doing in an organization – especially a government organization – pay a high price.

Self-interest versus communal interest

The utilitarian principle requires us to weigh up the costs and benefits to everyone who will be affected by a decision and then choose the option that brings the greatest total happiness. Generally this means we should blow the whistle if it helps people being saved from danger or abuse. But self-interest usually affects our choices.

> '*You either become complicit, or you challenge it.*'
>
> Michael Woodford, ex-president and CEO of Olympus who uncovered and revealed payments to Yakuza, the Japanese mafia, by high-ranking Olympus bosses

If you were in a sinking ship and could choose between saving your partner or two strangers, you would almost certainly save your partner. To make the altruistic decision to save the two strangers would be incomprehensible to others for its extreme (and some would say perverse) selflessness.

Accountancy of sacrifice

Some exploitative organizations and individuals depend on our self-interest to keep their bad practices hidden. A person who blows the whistle on an employer might lose their job or be persecuted at work. They might lose their workplace friendships and status.

Many whistle-blowers lose their homes, families, health and even lives in the subsequent stream of lawsuits and aggressive or vindictive responses. In some cases, their actions don't even achieve the result intended as the organization they have rumbled works to discredit the whistle-blower, who hasn't the resources to fight back. It takes an incredibly strong person with an unshakable sense of justice to rock the boat in this way.

Tribal loyalties

People tend to feel loyalty to any group to which they belong. Whistle-blowing entails a conflict of loyalties, because our commitment to the smaller, more immediate group (our co-workers and employers, for instance) is at odds with our loyalty to the larger community. When those who stand to benefit from the whistle-blowing are very remote from us – workers in a factory in Bangladesh, for instance – the cost to our more local 'tribe' might seem to outweigh the benefit to people we don't know and will never meet.

Conscience triumphs

When a whistle-blower takes the decision to come clean about some abuse or crime, they are following their conscience rather than a set of rules, guidelines or loyalties that would encourage

HERO OR TRAITOR?

American computer professional Edward Snowden released documents to the media revealing the extent of US surveillance of private citizens, including the use of data from Facebook and Google. He was accused of treason and fled the country. He is

quoted as saying: 'My sole motive is to inform the public as to that which is done in their name and that which is done against them.'

Is he a traitor, turning people against security measures that the government considers necessary, or a hero for standing up for the privacy and disclosure rights of law-abiding individuals?

His life is in ruins and he may serve a long term in jail. Was he a martyr or a fool to blow the whistle?

them to stay silent. According to evolutionary biologist Charles Darwin (1809–82), conscience evolved for precisely this reason – to help us resolve conflicts between self-interest and the interests of society in a manner that will aid the preservation of the whole community. On an individual level, it leads us to avoid behaviours which bring shame and are detrimental to society.

> 'Preserve a quiet conscience and you will always have joy. A quiet conscience can endure much, and remains joyful in all trouble, but an evil conscience is always fearful and uneasy.'
>
> Thomas à Kempis,
> *The Imitation of Christ,*
> c.1418

Whistle-blowers often end as martyrs. Chelsea (previously Bradley) Manning was sentenced to 35 years in prison for going public with documents and videos she had seen as a US soldier. These included footage of a US helicopter firing on unarmed civilians in Iraq in 2007.

Some philosophers, including St Thomas Aquinas (1225–74), see conscience as the application of practical reason. Others see it as given directly by God. Conscience is not always considered a rational faculty, but more a 'gut instinct' – although that may come about as a result of long-term indoctrination in a particular moral scheme. This results in the feeling that it would be 'right' to reveal abuse even though reason says it will probably have bad consequences for the whistle-blower. Indoctrination can cut

> **'The question of conscience is a matter for the head of the state, the sovereign.'**
>
> Adolf Eichmann, at his trial in Jerusalem, 1962

both ways, of course; when people employed by despotic regimes to oppress and torture others do not consider their actions to be wrong, it is clear that their consciences have deserted them.

> *'The private conscience is not only the last protection of the civilized world, it is the one guarantee of the dignity of man.'*
>
> Martha Gellhorn, 1962

CHAPTER 26

Is it better to give than receive?

For every gift, there must be a donor and a recipient. Is one better than the other?

Is it better to give than to receive? And if so, how much is it better to give? Who benefits more from charity – the donor or the recipient?

Giving because you want to or because you have to

One of the five pillars of Islam is 'zakah'. This is a duty to pay 2.5 per cent of your surplus wealth (money left after paying for essentials and taxes) as a contribution to help the poor. It serves two purposes – to make the Muslim reflect on the nature of wealth and avoid becoming too fond of material goods, and to redistribute wealth and help the poor. It is considered neither a tax nor a charitable donation. The penalty for non-contribution is severe: 'If any owner of gold or silver does not pay what is due on him, when the Day of Resurrection would come, plates of fire would be beaten out for him; these would then be heated in the fire of Hell and his sides, his forehead and his back would be cauterized with them. Whenever these cool down, (the process is) repeated during a day the extent of which would be fifty thousand years.'

Should we give money to homeless people living on the street? Or should we expect the state to provide for them?

In addition, Muslims are encouraged – but not obliged – to make donations to 'sadaqah', or charity. People with no religious or social obligation to give to the needy might still give generously to charity. They might feel they have a moral obligation to do so even though there is no formal imperative. Is there any difference in giving without obligation?

Values and duties

Philosophers often identify two different aspects of virtue: values and duties. Values are more open-ended and apply to states or people; duties are specific and relate to acts. So we could say that Gandhi was a virtuous man, and that helping an injured person is a social duty. There is often overlap, of course. A compassionate person will be more willing to discharge their duty to help someone who is injured. A duty may be an act one feels morally obliged to perform or one imposed by a rule.

The question then becomes – how much we should do?

Can you ever do enough?

If you decide to buy a hat or go on holiday or spend your time watching television, you are doing so at the expense of choosing to give your money and time to a charity. The charitable acts and donations would certainly bring greater total benefit than your new hat, holiday or watching TV for the evening, so charity is therefore the 'right' choice. But almost all of us don't and won't give up small personal gratifications to give everything we have to charity.

Two brands of consequentialism (the right or wrong, depending on the consequences of an act) help to salve our consciences and tell us our actions can be good enough, if not perfect. 'Progressive' consequentialism says we should act to make the world better than it would be if we did nothing, but we don't have to do everything we can to improve it. 'Satisficing' consequentialism says we should produce enough good – we don't have to give all to charity as long as we give some and we don't do harm with the time and money we are not giving.

Suppose a person has an income of $50,000 (£30,000). They want to help the poor. The obvious answer is for them to give their $50,000 away, but that won't really work. They will then be so poor that they will need the help of others in the form of donated food, shelter and clothing. So how would it be if they took out their necessary living costs and gave away the surplus? But now they don't have smart clothes and maybe won't be given a promotion that would come with a higher salary (which would make it easier for them to give away more of their money). Perhaps by maintaining a certain level of spending and socializing, they can associate with other wealthy people and persuade them to give to charity, too. A person who gives only $5,000 (£3,000) but encourages ten friends to give $2,000 (£1,200) each has contributed more than a person who gives $16,000 (£10,000).

Should you shave your head or grow a moustache?

Years ago, giving to charity was a private and usually anonymous act. It still can be – you can drop money into a collecting box, give anonymously online or by text message, or even endow a foundation that doesn't bear your name. But it's now increasingly common to make a public display of generosity. The boring old sponsored walk has been replaced by sponsored grow-a-moustache, sponsored head-shaving, sponsored abseiling and sponsored holidays (marathons in foreign countries, helping turtles into the sea on distant beaches, and so on).

Of course, no one will sponsor you for something if they don't know you're doing it. Shaving your head or growing a moustache is a very public act. The public display increases the funds raised for charity, but it also increases the exposure for your own generosity. It's very 'look at me'. Does that make any difference to the validity of the gesture? Or is it all the same, as long as the money comes in and goes to the needy? How much do the intentions and the gesture matter?

Practising virtue until it comes naturally

Aristotle would have liked us to act well because we are spurred on by virtue to do so, not in order for other people to be impressed by our generosity or so that we can feel good about ourselves. Natural feelings of compassion and generosity should make us want to help others with no thought for the effect it has on ourselves (as long as the effect is not so detrimental that it means we then need help from others). But what if you don't feel virtuous? Is it still good to give? It seems that it is.

The people on the receiving end of your good behaviour will benefit and you will be building up your virtue muscle by acting in the right way. Eventually, virtuous practice becomes ingrained and slowly automatic, if Jeremy Bentham was correct (see Chapter 24). It's a bit like taking exercise. You might really dislike it to start with, but after a while it becomes enjoyable and a part of your life. That, according to Aristotle, is when you count as virtuous – when acting virtuously is your default setting.

CHAPTER 27

To be, or not to be?

Is that the question?

'To be, or not to be?' asks Hamlet in his famous soliloquy in Shakespeare's play. The question is not simply whether suicide is justified or acceptable, but whether it is 'nobler' to live on with all the suffering that this may entail. It's not really a question to tackle in a moment of overwhelming personal crisis; it's one for a calmer, more contemplative mood.

God-given life

For many people, religious beliefs deny them the right to choose suicide. If your God has forbidden self-murder, and you accept the teachings of that God, the question doesn't arise. But there is always the question of what actually constitutes suicide, and this might be quite important to a person of faith.

> '*God's command "Thou shalt not kill," is to be taken as forbidding self-destruction.*'
>
> St Augustine, 345–430

A reasonable definition of suicidal behaviour would be that a person willingly and knowingly undertakes an action intended to kill themselves. We might allow it to be at one remove – so asking a doctor to administer a lethal dose of a drug could be suicide. On the other hand, running into a burning building in the hope of saving a child, but dying as a consequence, is not suicidal behaviour because the rescuer did not intend to die. Even though the person might know that death is a *likely* consequence, as it is not the *intended* consequence, it can't be called a suicide.

Accidentally taking an overdose of a prescription drug is not suicide, but taking it deliberately is suicide. Deliberately taking an overdose but taking too little to die is suicidal behaviour, but not suicide. Sometimes people make ambivalent suicide attempts. Do they actually want to die? Some suicides are probably failed suicidal gestures – in that, tragically, they fail to be a gesture and end in death. For the action to be suicide, intention, knowledge and outcome all have to come together (see Chapter 17).

It's not only religious believers who cite the sanctity of human life as a reason to rule out suicide. If we are to accept that human life is always special, no matter how much suffering it involves, the argument must logically be extended to ban all killing. That includes judicial execution, the shooting of an armed criminal threatening others, the slaughter of warfare, and letting someone in pain slip into death if they wish it rather than extending their life artificially. Few people are willing to sign up to a completely uncompromising position.

Putting up with it all

For the Ancient Greek philosophers, suicide was generally considered to be disgraceful. Plato suggested that suicides should be buried in unmarked graves. But he did allow some exceptions to this harsh attitude, including people suffering from madness, extreme torment, and shame at having acted immorally, not to mention the compulsion, in the Ancient Roman era, of judicial suicide.

For the Stoics, including Seneca (4BC–AD65), endurance was a virtue and led to a better life. They taught that we should try to accept what happens to us and respond with reason and moderation, qualities which are achieved by learning fortitude and self-control. The Stoics did not deny extreme emotional states, but sought to transform them and attain calm. According to Epictetus, the Stoic can be 'sick and yet happy, in peril and yet happy, dying and yet happy, in exile and happy, in disgrace and happy'.

The Stoic way did not rule out suicide, which was considered permissible in cases of extreme pain or disease, or if it was impossible, because of circumstances, to live a virtuous life (if one was oppressed by a tyrant, for instance). In other words, if a wise man, exercising reason, considered suicide to be the best option, it was permissible. As the Stoics considered some things essential to well-being, including health and freedom, lack of those could also be grounds for suicide. Seneca said that the wise man 'lives as long as he ought, not as long as he can'.

> '*Not only is suicide a sin, it is the sin. It is the ultimate and absolute evil, the refusal to take an interest in existence; the refusal to take the oath of loyalty to life. The man who kills a man, kills a man. The man who kills himself, kills all men. As far as he is concerned he wipes out the world.*'
>
> G. K. Chesterton, *Orthodoxy*, 1908

The problem of coercion

If a captured spy fears that she will be tortured, so takes a cyanide capsule, is it suicide? Assuming that the spy would not otherwise have sought to die, she has therefore been coerced into killing herself.

Must coercion be by a person? Someone with a painful terminal condition, who would not otherwise want to die, could say that they are coerced by circumstances. Most people

9/11: THE 'FALLING MAN' AND THE NOT-JUMPERS

On 11 September 2001, during the terrorist attack on New York, 200 people fell or jumped from the windows of the Twin Towers. The official record of the New York City medical examiner's office gives the cause of death as 'homicide by blunt trauma' (in other words, impact with the ground), not suicide. The victims are not listed as 'jumpers' because: 'Jumping indicates a choice, and these people did not have that choice. That is why the deaths were ruled homicide, because the actions of other people caused them to die.'

This account doesn't satisfy all the relatives of the deceased. For some, suicide is a sinful act which will bring divine retribution no matter what the circumstances. For others, the thought that their loved ones did have some control and were able to make one final choice, however terrible, is comforting. For those relatives, it is 'nobler in the mind' to end one's troubles.

who kill themselves do it to escape something – perhaps a terrible situation or mental anguish. If they could escape their torment without dying, they would probably do so.

Are they any more 'guilty' of suicide than the spy facing torture or the man who jumped from the North Tower of the World Trade Center on 9/11?

> '*When a man's circumstances contain a preponderance of things in accordance with nature, it is appropriate for him to remain alive; when he possesses or sees in prospect a majority of the contrary things, it is appropriate for him to depart from life.*'
>
> Cicero, 106–43BC

Thinking the unthinkable

For centuries, the prevailing view in Christian Europe was that suicide was an unpardonable sin. St Thomas Aquinas had three objections to it, one of which was the interesting notion that it is presumptuous – it takes the decision of when to end one's life out of God's hands and therefore usurps his authority. It was only after religion had begun to lose its stranglehold over Western thinking that philosophers could once again contemplate the concept of suicide without this accompanying ethos of inflexible cruelty.

The Ancient Greeks had considered suicide more in terms of social duty and duty to the gods than as a personal dilemma. David Hume addressed the social issue – one that still concerns people today – from a utilitarian standpoint. He proposed that if continuing with life is a painful burden for the individual, they are unlikely to be contributing a great deal to society, so the loss to society if that person dies is probably quite small and it is outweighed by the benefit to the individual in their release from it.

There are cases in which the utilitarian equation would argue against suicide – when it would leave grieving orphans to be cared for at public expense, perhaps. But some suicides

The Romantic movement, prevalent in Europe during the 19th century, glorified the idea of suicide as the inevitable response of the anguished soul disappointed in love or life.

may have little social impact – if the person leaves no surviving family, for example. In each case, the harm to the suicidal person of continuing to endure a life of anguish must be weighed against the harm to others (individuals or the community) to determine whether that particular suicide was morally wrong. Against the argument that suicide violates the social contract, the suicidal person could argue that society has already reneged on the agreement if life is intolerable for him or her.

In Ancient Greek legend, Sisyphus was a king whose punishment in Hades was to roll a huge rock up a mountain, only to have it rock back down again, for eternity.

Enduring the unendurable

The existentialists, famous for smoking and drinking coffee in Parisian cafés in the 20th century, identified the 'absurd' fact that human life is meaningless, there is no God, no purpose to what we do, and that ultimately all is vanity and death. This theory is called 'absurd' not because it's ridiculous, but because it renders life and the search for meaning absurd. The anxiety, or angst that comes from the recognition of our impotence and insignificance is a deep philosophical despair.

So – if it's all going to end in tears anyway, why not end it all now? The conclusion that life is therefore pointless is one which Albert Camus struggled to avoid. In the end, he said, we have to live in spite of that knowledge: 'The struggle itself is enough to fill a man's heart.'

Using the analogy of Sisyphus, condemned forever in Greek myth to push a heavy boulder up a mountain and then have it roll back down again, Camus concluded that the way forward is to 'imagine Sisyphus happy' – that is, to accept the situation and find it liberating and enjoy living within the freedom it gives us.

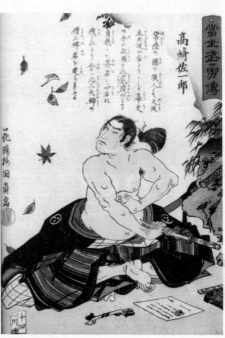

For a Japanese samurai defeated in battle, shamed or condemned to death, ritual suicide by self-inflicted disembowelling was a moral duty. Known as sepukku or hara-kiri, it was performed by cutting across the abdomen using a special knife.

Suicide as a duty

Philosopher John Hardwig makes a controversial claim that in some cases people have a moral obligation to kill themselves. If their continuing life is so burdensome to others that ending it would produce greater benefit in total than continuing, they should opt for suicide. However, he does concede: 'I can readily imagine that, through cowardice, rationalization, or failure of resolve, I will fail in this obligation to protect my loved ones.'

(There is no) conclusion

Philosophy is an unending endeavour. Once you start to think about the myriad questions that life throws up, it's impossible to stop. Even if you reach answers to some of the questions, you will always find more questions to ask. But the one, truly important question everyone should address is, 'what do I think?' Everything follows from that. To return again to Kierkegaard: 'The thing is to find a truth which is true for [you], to find the idea for which [you] can live and die.'

Philosophy is a quest for truth. If we see it as a quest for absolute truth, we won't get to the end of the journey – but that's not the same as failing. If we see it as a quest for 'a truth which is true for [you]', you just might reach the end of your journey. You might even recognize it when you get there.

And we should give the last word to Sophocles, who set the ball rolling for Western philosophy. Remember, 'The unexamined life is not worth living.'

PICTURE CREDITS